Fat Cats, High Rollers, and Banksters

By

C. Foster Stanback

Fat Cats, High Rollers, and Banksters
Copyright © 2013
Foster Stanback
Cover design by Jonathan Stanback

All rights reserved. No part of the publication may be reproduced, stored in a retrieval system, or transmitted to any form or by any means—electronic, mechanical, photocopying, recording, or otherwise—without the prior written permission of the author and publisher. The only exception is brief quotations in printed or online reviews.

Published by Lulu®
www.lulu.com

Printed in the United States of America

ISBN-978-1-105-09904-5

Preface

The once prosperous American economy, where everyone had an ample opportunity to make a decent living, has become a big casino. The fat cats, high rollers, and banksters have rigged all the games so that they cash in while everyone else loses their shirts. The essays collected in this book provide insights into how the capitalist system works in the present era—and how you can navigate it to take control of your personal financial destiny.

Table Of Contents

Chapter 1
It's the End of the World as We Knew It
9

Chapter 2
Ken Lay and Executive Pay
41

Chapter 3
Corporate Morlocks
53

Chapter 4
GDP and Me
57

Chapter 5
Nation Slaves
63

Chapter 6
The Politics of Persuasion
67

Chapter 7
The Welfare State
71

Chapter 8
The New Sparta
75

Chapter 9
The Golden Rule
79

Chapter 10
Rat-proofing Your Portfolio
83

Chapter 11
The Sausage Factory
91

Chapter 12
Sleaze and Fees
97

Chapter 13
Thanksgiving: The Rest of the Story
103

Chapter 14
Housing Hokum
109

Chapter 15
Student Loans: Leave Them Alone
113

Chapter 16
Don't Bet the Farm
117

Chapter 17
How To Avoid Getting Hacked, Jacked, or Whacked: A Brief Guide To Personal Financial Security
121

Chapter 1

It's The End Of The World As We Knew It

For Americans who grew up during the Cold War, the dismantling of the communist state in the Soviet Union and the Soviet Bloc countries brought a triumphant relief from the daily anxiety of living under the constant threat of mutually assured destruction. Yet at the same time, this "victory" in the Cold War brought on a new sense of apprehension about what the future might hold. Previously, one's focus could be more easily diverted from the structural deficiencies of the "Free World" due to the presence of a dangerous enemy propelled by an inferior ideology. Now, however, it is much more difficult to avoid noticing the serious flaws of our own system. All around us we see the contradictory signs of a post-war devastation mingled with those of a post-war boom. Abandoned, dilapidated factories and businesses in the inner cities resemble the destruction left from an aerial bombardment. Homeless, displaced families can be found wandering the streets of America's urban centers. Middle class factory workers now work long hours at fast-food restaurants just to eek out a living. College graduates, who at one time would have readily obtained lucrative employment, now compete with each other for low-paying clerical jobs. Enormous debt, normally the burden borne by countries that have been defeated in a war, now plagues the nation as a whole as well as the majority of individuals. Signs such as these are not the result of some sudden economic catastrophe or a radical political upheaval, but rather the effects of a recurring process in the development of capitalism as a world system.

The history of capitalism has been characterized by the rise of dominant regimes of accumulation that are inevitably superseded by competing regimes. Since the emergence of the capitalist system in the Middle Ages, four successive regimes of accumulation have risen to a position of dominance over the world economy: the Genoese, the Dutch, the British, and the Americans. Each new regime has been characterized by greater size, complexity, and power and functioned to extend the boundaries of capitalism's influence. On the other hand, the time taken by each regime to rise to dominance and then decline has been steadily decreasing. A historical analysis of these regimes of accumulation reveals a number of patterns that appear to be part of recurring cycles characteristic of the capitalist world system. If such an analysis proves to be correct, then capitalist history may well be reaching a critical turning point in which the hegemony of the American cycle of accumulation is coming to a close and a new regime will emerge.

The capitalist system, in its modern form, arose during Age of Exploration in response to the greatly increased market for European goods. The guild-masters of the feudal system were replaced by large-scale manufacturers who produced items that they could sell in new foreign markets, such as America, East India, and China. Many of these goods were manufactured from raw materials brought in from European-controlled colonies located throughout the world. Steam-power and machinery launched the manufacturing process to new heights of production with the advent of the Industrial Age. Tremendous technological advances in transportation and communication generated an even greater efficiency in the markets as well as greater profits for European industrial giants.

During this period, productive capacity became so great that Karl Marx predicted that the problem of *overproduction* would ultimately lead to capitalism's demise. He claimed that "modern bourgeois society with its relations of production, of exchange and of property, a society that has conjured up such gigantic means of production and of exchange, is like the sorcerer who is no longer able to control the powers of the nether world whom he has called up by his spells" (Marx and Engels 46-49). In spite of the numerous boom and bust cycles that have continued to occur over the years, the most devastating for Americans being the Great Depression of the 1930s, the final crisis for capitalism has not arrived. On the contrary, the power of profit maximization to organize the productive forces of society has virtually eliminated any serious consideration of alternatives by governing entities in every part of the world.

The capitalist system is defined by its treatment of *commodities*, or the products that humans produce in order to survive. Instead of producing for themselves or their immediate associates, people produce for someone else—the capitalist. The capitalist, whether an individual, a group of individuals, or the state, provides the *means of production* for the worker. These means of production may consist of such things as technical knowledge, tools, machinery, raw materials, or a suitable working area. The things that are produced are then exchanged in the *market* for money. This money can then be used by the capitalist to buy other things, such as new equipment or more raw materials, which can then be used to produce more things to be sold for even more money. The cycle repeats itself endlessly as long as the capitalist continues to make more money from the sale of the things produced than he was required to spend on the equipment, raw materials, and labor to produce them. In other words, as long as a *profit* is made on goods produced, the capitalist will continue to produce more. As one can readily see, such a system contains no inherent incentive to increase the wages of the worker as profits are made on the goods produced, since as long as the worker is willing to work, greater profits can only be achieved by spending current profits on new equipment or more raw materials.

The operating principle of capitalism, *profit maximization*, has two consequences. The first is competition. People will inevitably compete with each other to obtain greater profits on the goods and services available to sell. As more and more people compete to sell a limited number of items, they will inevitably search for new things that can be transformed into commodities to be bought, sold, or rented. This process, called *commodification*, is the second consequence of profit maximization. Because of commodification, things such as drinking water, which was previously considered a resource freely available to all, have been marketed and sold for a profit. Human labor has also become a commodity, with capitalists searching the world over for the cheapest workers available to manufacture their goods.

Capitalists will adopt two strategies in order to successfully compete in the marketplace against other capitalists. The first is to reinvest their profits in the business. This concentration strategy allows a particular capitalist entity to gain a greater dominance over others. A second strategy aimed at increasing market dominance is centralization. Profits from operations can be used to eliminate the competition by buying up smaller companies. The larger a company grows, the more difficult it becomes for smaller companies to compete with it. Bigger companies are able to demand lower prices from suppliers because their orders are larger. Bigger manufacturing companies will have greater economies of scale. Companies can also integrate vertically by buying up all of their suppliers. At the extreme level a company may buy up other companies at every stage of its production process, as did Rockefeller's Standard Oil Company before it was broken up by antitrust legislation. Centralization can also occur when companies integrate horizontally by forming *mergers* with other unrelated companies.

The process of centralization has now expanded to a global level with the formation of extremely large and powerful transnational corporations. Some of these corporations have a yearly income greater than the Gross Domestic Product of many nations. They have utilized their enormous economic power to influence the global political process and create a worldwide market for their goods and services. Entire countries have been transformed into export platforms, supplying the raw materials and human labor to produce the products that these companies then sell in the global marketplace.

Profit maximization as the principle of social organization cannot occur unless two other conditions are satisfied. First of all, it requires a supportive political system. Such a system was described by Senator Bois

Penrose of Pennsylvania in the following manner: "I believe in the division of labor. You send us to Congress; We pass the laws under which you make money... and out of your profits you further contribute to our campaign funds to send us back again to pass more laws to enable you to make more money"(Araghi, *Social Change*).

A second condition necessary for capitalism to flourish is an idealogical system that legitimizes it. As wealth is inevitably concentrated into the hands of a few while more and more people suffer deprivation, a system of illusions must be created that will sustain social inequalies by misrepresenting them. In the United States, this ideology denies the existence of a class system; in India the class system is an integral part of the society's religion.

From its beginnings, capitalism has depended on political and idealogical support structures for its development. During the Age of Exploration, new markets were kept open by European warships sent by mercantilist governments. Northern Europe, which was largely Protestant, developed a stronger capitalist system than Spain and Portugal due in part to the powerful ideological support structure of the *Protestant Ethic*. Traditionally, the pursuit of profit had been viewed by society as a selfish act motivated by greed. Protestantism succeeded in reversing this view and turning profit into a moral crusade. The *Protestant Ethic* emerged from the theological ideas of John Calvin.

Calvin, one of the key leaders of the Protestant Reformation, believed that only a few people were chosen for salvation. Everyone was predestined at birth to be among the saved or the damned and there was nothing an individual could do to change his or her fate. To reduce the anxiety that they would naturally feel about their eternal destiny, believers were encouraged to look for signs in their lives which would indicate they were among the saved. One of the key signs of salvation, according to Calvinists, was prosperity. Such a belief system led to a number of consequences for the development of the capitalist spirit. First of all, capitalists could mercilessly pursue economic success while believing they were fulfilling their ethical duty. They also had access to loyal employees who would work diligently at a job in fulfillment of their life purpose, even if they were being exploited. Finally, the Protestant Ethic legitimized the new unequal class system of bourgeois and worker that was emerging to replace the old feudal order (Ritzer 149-150).

The development of the capitalist economic system can be divided into four cycles of accumulation over the past six hundred years: the Genoese cycle (15th to early 17th Century), the Dutch cycle (late 16th to late 18th Century), the British cycle (mid 18th Century to early 20th Century), and the American cycle (late 19th Century to present). Each of these cycles has overlapped as succeeding regimes rose to a position of dominance over their predecessors. Also, each cycle, while lasting more than a century, has been progressively shorter in duration. All four cycles have consisted of two distinct phases: a phase of material expansion in which money capital was used to acquire or produce an increasing amount of commodities that were then used to acquire even more money capital; and a period of financial expansion in which money capital was redirected from investment in commodities to financial deals in order to procure greater profits (Arrighi 6).

This second phase of accumulation occurs when the profits from the investment of money capital in the expansion of trade and production are reduced due to an intensification of inter-capitalist competition (Arrighi 88). As long as trade was continuing to expand, there was plenty of room for newcomers to enter a market and find a niche. Even when a number of capitalists were operating in the same line of business, their competition only served to open up new sources of supply and new outlets for their products. Yet as capitalists accumulated more money than they could profitably invest within their own market niches, they began to invest instead in the hostile takeover of their competitors' markets. Inter-capitalist competition became a matter of driving others out of business rather than cooperating and dividing profits. Once this point was reached, accumulated profits were redirected to more promising financial markets and the second phase of accumulation began (Arrighi 90-94). This second phase of financial expansion has proven to be the herald signaling the maturation of one cycle of accumulation and the beginning of a new one (Arrighi 87).

The switch from trade and production to financial intermediation and speculation reflects an attempt by an economic regime's capitalist class to maintain its position of dominance over world markets once the point of diminishing returns has been reached. The switch does in fact bring on a temporary period of renewed wealth and power for the regime's capitalist class, which Giovanni Arrighi has deemed a "wonderful moment" in the systemic cycle of accumulation. The "wonderful moment" is not shared by the nation as a whole, however, and only forestalls the ultimate demise of the regime as the hegemonic leader of the world capitalist system (Arrighi 215).

Until the late 14th Century, the Italian city-state of Genoa had been a chief rival of Venice in the lucrative trade of the eastern Mediterranean. Yet after a series of wars that finally ended with the Peace of Turin in 1381, Venice succeeded in ousting Genoa from these markets. Genoa had already suffered from an increasing loss of trade revenues during the earlier part of the century. The total value of merchandise entering the port of Genoa dropped from 4,000,000 Genoese pounds in 1293 to 2,000,000 pounds in 1334 and seldom rose above the latter amount during the rest of the century (Arrighi 90-91).

Once investment in trade no longer proved to be profitable, Genoese capital was used instead to finance the increasing public debts of the Italian city-states (Arrighi 109). By the 15th Century, Genoese merchant bankers had found an even more advantageous outlet for their surplus capital in the newly formed nation-state of Spain, which was opening up vast new commercial space as it strove to expand its territories (Arrighi 121). The financial expansion of the Genoese lasted for several hundred years and enabled them to dominate European high finance. Yet even during its height a new cycle of capital accumulation had already begun with the Dutch nation, a regime that would ultimately replace the Genoese as the leading financial power of Europe.

When Spanish troops landed in the Netherlands in

1566 to enforce taxation, Dutch rebels refined their maritime skills through piracy and privateering against Spain. During the eighty-year period of struggle before the Dutch nation was recognized, the country's wealth and power expanded through control over supplies of grain and naval stores from the Baltic region (Arrighi 132). Surplus capital from the Baltic trade was utilized to transform Amsterdam into the center for storage and exchange of the most important commodities of European and world trade. In addition, Amsterdam became the key money and capital market of the European colonial powers. This was accomplished in part by establishing the first stock exchange to remain in session on a permanent basis. Eventually the Amsterdam stock exchange began to attract surplus capital from all over Europe, giving the Dutch a supreme command over liquid assets in addition to commodities.

Finally, the Dutch government chartered large joint-stock companies which held the exclusive rights to enormous overseas commercial territories. Although these were business enterprises, they were endowed with the ability to perform war-making and state-making functions on behalf of the government, and thus became important instruments of the global expansion of Dutch commercial and financial power (Arrighi 137-139). One such chartered company, the VOC (*Verenigde OosteIndische Compagnie*), became the vanguard of Dutch commercial and military power in the east Indies. The VOC became increasingly involved in military operations and territorial conquests in order to protect its monopoly of trade in this region. Yet this policy greatly inflated the protection costs of the Dutch empire as local peoples rebelled against their rule and other European mercantilist powers began to compete for control of the lucrative overseas commercial territories (Arrighi 141-142, 156-157).

In addition, an increasing percentage of the profits from the VOC's operations was diverted from the shareholders to expanding the bureaucratic structure of the company and rewarding the top management. A similar pattern can be seen in many American corporations toward the end of the twentieth century and the early part of the twenty-first century (Arrighi 157). From about 1740 onward, the Dutch capitalist class began to withdraw from trade and specialize in supplying the enormous credit needs of the competing European colonial powers. Eventually, the Dutch were drawn into the very struggles they were profiting from, taking sides with France in a war against the British. In spite of suffering initial defeats, Britain eventually retaliated by destroying Dutch maritime power in the fourth Anglo-Dutch war of 1781-84. The final blow to Dutch hegemony came during the Napoleonic Wars when the nation disappeared from the map of Europe and London replaced Amsterdam as the seat of world commercial and financial power (Arrighi 142-143).

England had begun its process of capital accumulation even before the Dutch nation had achieved its independence. King Henry VIII, in spite of accessing the vast local revenues of the Catholic church by breaking off relations with Rome, quickly squandered these funds in unsuccessful military campaigns. He finally resorted to obtaining loans by force and debasing the currency, plunging the nation into social unrest and political instability. As a result, England lost its last territory on the European continent, the French port of Calais. England's misfortunes were soon reversed, however, with the rise of Elizabeth I. She avoided the costly continental wars of her father and instead consolidated her power in the British Isles. She built up the royal navy and focused on expanding overseas territories. In addition, she supported piracy and privateering against Spain. Britain's superior seapower was ultimately confirmed by the defeat of the Spanish Armada in 1588.

Capital accumulated from privateering was used in the establishment of joint-stock companies, such as the East India Company, the Royal African Company, and the Hudson Bay Company, which were instrumental in advancing England's commercial power (Arrighi 184-187). Besides the advantageous geographical endowment of being located at the crossroads of Baltic, Asian, and American trade, Britain possessed large deposits of iron and coal. Thus, the nation was ideally suited to become the birthplace of the Industrial Revolution, which would allow capital accumulation to occur at an unprecedented rate. The iron industry supplied the insatiable demand for machinery, railways, and ships used to manufacture and transport British capital goods to the domestic and foreign markets. Money capital was quickly converted into commodities as the entire world economy became linked to London.

Yet this enormous expansion of production and trade inevitably reached a point of diminishing returns as competitive pressures among capitalists increased, culminating in the Great Depression of 1873-96 (Arrighi 160-163). As in the Genoese and Dutch cycles of accumulation, British capitalists began to redirect their resources from trade and production to finance in order to achieve greater returns. The latter part of the 19th Century was marked by a massive exodus of capital from Britain, much of which found its way to the rapidly rising economic regime of the United States. This period also witnessed an enormous expansion of British banking networks (Arrighi 165). The switch to financial enterprises resulted in a "wonderful moment" of prosperity from the years 1896-1914. Yet this moment was not shared by Britain's working class and it was short-lived (Arrighi 173). Although Britain was victorious in World War I, the second world war would bring about the dismantling of the British empire and the establishment of the United States as the new global economic power.

The American cycle of accumulation has been distinguished by the innovation of large vertically integrated enterprises which encompassed both the processes of mass production as well as mass distribution, resulting in a reduction of the transaction costs of goods from primary production to final consumption. Cash flows generated from these highly efficient enterprises were reinvested in the businesses to employ hierarchies of managers to monitor and regulate markets and labor functions. The massive organizational structures created formidable barriers to entry for competitors. These enterprises were also afforded the opportunity to expand in a protected, continental-sized market (Arrighi 239-241).

The greatest challenge to the profitability of large American firms came not from competitors, but from the labor they employed. This challenge was effectively met by new organizational innovations which further strengthened their power over workers. Although various labor movements arose in the United States toward the end of the 19th century, they were normally forced underground by a government more supportive of business interests. Nevertheless, business leaders sensed the growing pressure from discontented workers and took measures to protect their position of power.

One of their key strategies was to adopt the scientific management formula devised by F.W. Taylor. This formula involved organizing the production process so that it would not depend upon the knowledge and craftsmanship of the laborer. Assembly was broken down into isolated, repetitive movements. Numerous time and motion studies were undertaken in order to extract the maximum output from each worker. Those aspects of production which had previously depended on individual problem-solving were moved from the factory floor to the planning department. The idea behind the formula was that management would have a monopoly over every aspect of the process of production. Workers would be effectively de-skilled and become easily replaceable in the event of a strike.

At the beginning of the 20th century, Henry Ford combined the principles of Taylorism with mass production techniques such as automated assembly lines in the manufacture of automobiles. Fordism soon became the industrial norm, but the large factories were highly susceptible to the problem of overproduction, resulting in lower wages for workers and massive layoffs. The social necessity for workers movements to protect them from economic downturns brought on by the capitalist system became more and more apparent. The communist revolution in Russia gave impetus to the growing popularity of similar movements in the United States. The government, however, continued to support business interests and utilized force when necessary to quell popular demonstrations for workers' rights.

All this changed with the onset of The Great Depression. So many people were without work, homes, and food that public unrest began to pose a serious threat to capitalism itself. At that point the traditional laissez-faire policy of the government was abandoned and numerous reforms were enacted to provide jobs and economic security for the worker. Ideological support for the new policies was found in the views of British economist Milton Keynes, who claimed that market forces must be moderated by government intervention in the economy if the boom-bust cycles of capitalism were to be avoided. Keynes advocated raising the wages of workers so that they would be able to buy what they produced, thereby creating a need for continued production and eliminating mass layoffs. The *Keynesian Revolution* lasted from 1930 to 1975, when the government began a return to the policies of the previous era in response to pressure from business interests. Meanwhile, capitalists found sufficient room for profit-taking in the enormous production required to support America's involvement in World War II and in the post-war economic boom.

After the war, the principles of Fordism expanded around the world. Two dominant profit-maximizing systems began vying for control of the global market.

One was the United States. The other was the Soviet Union. The United States promoted a "free enterprise system" in which the means of production were privately owned. The Soviet Union promoted a "state enterprise system" in which the means of production were government-owned. The *market share* controlled by the United States included western Europe and some Third World nations. The Soviet Union controlled eastern Europe and a limited number of countries in the Third World. The basic capitalistic principle of maximizing profits was followed by both systems. In the free enterprise system profits accrued in the form of money to the individuals and stockholders who controlled the production process. In the state enterprise system profits accrued in the form of fringe benefits and material goods to the controlling elites in the government.

The strategy of combining de-skilled human labor with mass production techniques to maximize profits was utilized by both systems. Both systems were also controlled by a group of elites who utilized the state to promote their economic interests. In the United States this state support of business interests took the form of numerous invasions by US forces into Third World nations where markets were threatened, such as Vietnam and various Latin American countries. In the Soviet Union military forces were utilized to keep their markets open in places such as Hungary, Poland, and Afghanistan.

Both the American and Soviet systems were supported by a strong ideological framework. The most salient doctrine of the American system was *freedom*. This freedom was couched in the lore of the

Revolutionary War and enshrined in such documents as the *Declaration of Independence*, the *Constitution*, and the *Bill of Rights*. American military forces were defined for the public as the heroic defenders of this cherished freedom, both for Americans and other peoples who lived abroad. Freedom for Americans was expressed both politically and economically in the right to vote and the right to engage in individual profit-making activities, even though political decisions and the "free" market were ultimately controlled by elites. The United States continued to use the term "capitalism" and associate it with freedom of economic opportunity. In spite of the increased concentration of wealth into the hands of a diminishing proportion of the population, the existence of a class system was formally denied.

At the heart of the Soviet system lay the doctrine of *equality*. The underlying capitalist structure of the system was denied and the term *communism* was utilized to define the Soviet Union as a system which embodied the philosophy of Karl Marx. The idea of equality was couched in the lore of the Bolshevik Revolution and enshrined in such documents as the *Communist Manifesto*. The Soviet military and its latest hardware were frequently paraded through the streets of Moscow as the defenders against "Yankee Imperialism." Equality for the Soviets was expressed politically in their right to vote and economically in their right to state-provided jobs, healthcare, and schools. In reality, the equality was only a myth, since the ruling elites picked their own successors and had access to much greater material benefits than the public at large. The different ideological systems operating in the Soviet Union and the United

States were so strong that they eventually superseded the economic competition between the two countries and generated the much deeper hostility of the Cold War.

Ultimately, the Soviet system failed, as most weaker entities do in the competitive marketplace of capitalism. The Soviet Union began as an agrarian, semi-feudal society with an extremely small industrial base. Although tremendous progress was made during the 20th Century, the system was never able to catch up to the industrially superior power of the United States. Any market taken over by the Soviet Union, such as the eastern Bloc countries, had to be closed off from the outside since the inferior products produced in the Soviet Union's fledgling factories would not have been able to compete with the goods produced in the advanced factories of the United States and the West.

From 1945 until 1973 the capitalist system of the United States expanded the principles of Fordism to a global level. American corporations, having already acquired experience in growing their markets over large geographic areas through interstate commercial ventures, were in a prime position to assert their dominance in the global marketplace. The government supported business interests with policies such as the Marshall Plan, which provided U.S. government credits to the devastated nations of Europe for rebuilding with American machinery and other goods.

Following the war, the bulk of the world's manufacturing capability, along with the capacity for technological research and development, was now based in the United States. This already considerable infrastructure was further expanded by the Cold War, enabling America's corporate giants to dedicate huge sums of money to the development and manufacture of new technologies with the assurance of continued purchases by the government. Not surprisingly, American companies were responsible for 100 of the major technological innovations between 1945 and 1960, including the transistor and integrated circuits, which made possible a number a number of profitable consumer products in addition to military hardware (Pollard 132-133).

U.S. hegemony of the global marketplace went unchallenged until the early 1970s. By that time Japan and the nations of Europe had fully recovered their former industrial might and began to compete against the United States. The new competition in the international marketplace resulted in a profitability crisis for American corporations. To bolster diminishing profits, low level assembly jobs were exported overseas where factories could take advantage of much lower labor costs.

Unions, which previously had been able to wield the threat of a strike in order to obtain concessions from management, found themselves in a rather precarious position. Instead of bargaining to obtain better wages and benefits for workers, they now had to offer wage and benefit reductions to management in an effort to persuade companies not to move their operations overseas. If corporations initiated cuts in pay or benefits, unions had no choice but to concede or face a plant shutdown. In an ironic reversal, the weapon of halting operations, once called a strike and utilized by unions to obtain concessions from management, was now called a plant shutdown and used by management to obtain concessions from the unions.

As manufacturing jobs left the country, the United States underwent a transformation from an industrial economy to a service economy. Traditional blue-collar factory jobs that paid a middle class wage and provided health insurance and retirement benefits began to be replaced by low paying jobs in service industries such as the fast-food business. To avoid paying benefits and giving raises, workers were hired on a temporary basis or only allowed to work part-time. The lower wages of the service industry often required both parents to work in order to support a family. If one wage earner became temporarily or permanently unemployed, family income was not sufficient to pay the mortgage or the rent, resulting in another addition to the growing ranks of the homeless.

Service sector wages were kept low by a continual influx of illegal immigrants who could easily replace any citizens who were unwilling to work for such meager pay. Business owners whose profit-making activity was bound to American shores utilized institutions such as the U.S. Chamber of Commerce to fight immigration enforcement so that they could keep wages depressed. Even simple measures, such as requiring businesses to verify the legal status of new hires, have been continually blocked in Congress (Mann).

American business interests sought further relief from the growing profit squeeze by lobbying the government for tax reforms designed to lower the taxes levied on corporations and investors. Reforms were initiated during the Carter administration but progressed rapidly once Ronald Reagan took office. Tax breaks for corporations resulted in reduced revenues for the national treasury. Many corporations paid much more in foreign taxes than in local taxes. Tax rates for wealthy individuals were reduced as well, from 94% in the 1950s to the current cap of 39.6%.

Lowering taxes for the wealthy resulted in the largest redistribution of wealth in U.S. history. From the end of WWII until the late 1970s, incomes were becoming more equal. In 1976 the top 1 percent of households received 8.9 percent of all pre-tax income; by the late 2000s this share had increased to 21 percent. According the U.S. Census, the incomes of the top 5 percent of Americans increased 72.7 percent from 1979 to 2009 while the incomes of the bottom 20 percent decreased 7.4 percent (Inequality.org). Once inflation is taken into account, a young American male now makes 12 percent less than what his father made 30 years ago (Stiglitz).

Even though revenues for the federal coffers had been drastically reduced by cutting taxes for the rich, the government continued to spend enormous amounts of money on the defense budget, once again with prompting by business interests seeking bolstered profits from military contracts. After spending more than $13 trillion in the post-WWII period to win the Cold War, US military expenditures continued to rise even in the absence of a Soviet threat. Clinton spent more on the military than Richard Nixon did in 1975 and almost as much as Lyndon Johnson did in 1965, presiding over a defense budget triple that of Moscow and almost double that of France, Germany, and Japan combined (Bandow). George W. Bush pushed defense spending into overdrive by launching two disastrous wars into Iraq and

Afghanistan. At a burn rate of $12 billion per month, these excursions are projected to reach a total cost of $4-6 trillion once the final tab comes in (Londono, Hanley).

Reduced tax revenues coupled with the spending increases of the military-industrial complex led to the enormous federal budget deficit that has now become a national crisis. Business leaders, unwilling to cede any of the ground they had gained, instead found a scapegoat in government programs such as Aid To Families With Dependent Children, popularly termed "welfare." Stereotypes such as "freeloaders" and "welfare queens" were touted as the real culprits in the budget crisis in order to gain middle class support for program cuts. These ideas seemed to be gaining traction, but the elites suffered a considerable setback when their presidential candidate Mitt Romney extended the blame for America's financial woes to the middle class as well, claiming that 47 percent of Americans were freeloaders (Corn).

While America's poor and middle class struggled to make ends meet, wealthy individuals and corporations poured their tax windfall into the financial markets. The new influx of money fueled an unprecedented rise in the stock market and provided funds for the expansion of the booming credit industry. The federal government, foreign governments, and millions of individuals eagerly submitted themselves to a yoke of debt in order to escape the effects of the economic crisis. Individuals who resisted indebting themselves usually succumbed to the bombardment of television and mail offers for credit cards.

Foreign governments desiring loans for development

were required to submit themselves to the policies of the World Bank and the International Monetary Fund, organizations that served as agents for the industrial masters of the First World. These institutions functioned much like collection agencies, forcing the debtor countries to make repayments on their outstanding loans by whatever means necessary.

Since the average citizens of the lower income countries were 55 times poorer than the average citizens of the developed creditor nations, extracting enough hard currency to make loan repayments could only be accomplished by implementing rigid austerity programs that eliminated public sector spending on vital services such as basic healthcare and education, thereby deepening the plight of people already living at little more than a subsistence level (George xv). In places such as Africa, countries reduced expenditures on public healthcare by as much as 50%, causing infant mortality rates to double. Government expenditures on education in this region were reduced by 25% (Araghi, "World Bank" 1).

The result of these structural adjustments imposed by the World Bank and the IMF was an ironic flow of resources from the underdeveloped nations of the Third World to the wealthier industrialized nations of the First World. From 1982 to 1990 the total capital inflows to the Third World were $927 billion. Outflows of capital from the Third World to the First World to service debts, on the other hand, were $1345 billion. Thus, the net transfer of resources to the First World amounted to $418 billion, a number that did not include other capital transfers in the form of royalties, dividends, repatriated profits, and underpaid raw materials. In 1948 the United States transferred $14 billion ($70 billion in 1991 dollars) to help rebuild Europe after the devastation of World War II. From 1982-90 the economically devastated nations of the world transferred the equivalent of six Marshall Plans to the wealthy nations of the First World. Yet after nearly a decade of enormous debt-servicing payments and rigidly-implemented austerity programs, the indebted nations of the world began the 1990s sixty-one per cent more in debt than they were in 1982. The debt of the least developed countries had increased by 110 percent (George xiv-xvi).

The burden of the debts was felt most by the poorest citizens of these nations who had to accept lower wages and reduced public services. The uppermost level of society remained relatively insulated from the negative effects of the debt crisis, since they could shelter their assets in foreign bank accounts and take advantage of the low wages to acquire cheap labor to employ in their businesses and households. Reduced public services were not missed since they could afford to acquire private ones (George xvii).

In addition to public sector austerity programs, the IMF and the World Bank required the debtor nations to implement structural adjustments in their economies that would align them with the development model created by the already industrialized nations. The First World powers, which had protected their fledgling industries with trade barriers until they had fully developed, now obliged the debtor nations of the Third World to keep their markets open by signing agreements such as the General Agreement on Trade and Tariffs and the North

American Free Trade Agreement. Third World nations, unable to compete in the marketplace with industrial goods, had no choice but to become export platforms for raw materials and cheap labor in service to the First World industrial powers. As agricultural production was shifted to cash crops grown on large farms, poorer farmers were displaced from their lands and forced to settle on the periphery of the large urban centers and compete for an insufficient number of low wage jobs in the factories serving the export industry. Those not able to find employment would have to turn to crime or the informal economy. Currently in the world there are 197,000,000 people who are unemployed and 397,000,000 of those lucky enough to be working live in extreme poverty (Orhanghazi).

Although the switch to export-led agricultural production was promoted as "agricultural reform" and supported by post-mercantilist/neo-Ricardian economic theories emphasizing specialization in the global market instead of national development, the results of such policies further widened the gap between the rich and the poor in these nations. The "reforms" were accomplished by deregulating the industry and allowing world market demand rather than the government direct the course of agricultural production. Theoretically, the change should have brought about a more efficient allocation of resources, eventually benefitting everyone; In reality, however, this was not the case (Araghi, "Global Depeasantization" 356).

Market theory, useful as it may be, has a number of limitations which are overlooked by many of those who promote it with an almost religious fervor. First of all, the market, if left to its own devices, only perpetuates previously existing inequalities in wealth and income. It is financially rather than morally driven and is completely blind to the social and resource costs of production. Also, in the absence of social constraints placed on it, the market leads to the concentration of economic power in the hands of a few. When the principle of "survival of the fittest" is given free reign in society, those with greater economic power end up controlling or exploiting those with less (Lappe, *World Hunger* 78-80).

Farshaad Araghi supplies a useful corollary to market theory as applied to deregulation in the agricultural industry: "nonintervention on the part of the state is in fact a form of intervention, because the existing inequalities of wealth and power will in practice make the rich—rather than the masses of near-subsistence peasants/workers—the main beneficiaries of deregulation" (Araghi, "Global Depeasantization" 356). As agricultural production in undeveloped nations was entrusted to the care of the world market through deregulation, devastation soon followed: Local staple foods were no longer produced in sufficient quantities to support the population, resulting in widespread hunger and malnutrition. The yearly death toll for those falling victim to hunger now stands at 18 to 20 million people—more than double the number who died each year during World War II (Lappe, *World Hunger* 3).

In response to the growing economic calamity the marginalized populations of the world resorted to the only means available to them to attain some measure of economic security: having more children. While such reasoning may seem strange to a citizen of an industrialized nation where economic security is generated by such devices as social security and pension funds, to someone in the Third World children often provide the only means of survival when the household breadwinner becomes too old or too sickly to work. Eighty to ninety percent of the people surveyed in the nations of Indonesia, South Korea, Thailand, and Turkey plan to depend on their children to support them in old age (Lappe, *Population* 22).

Studies conducted in some of the world's poorest countries have shown that in the rural economy, children begin to contribute more than they consume by the time they have reached adolescence (Lappe, *Population* 21). In urban areas children contribute economically to the family through "sibling assistance chains." Each successive child that completes school is in a position to help support the next one to climb higher on the educational ladder and get a higher paying job.

Also, a "lottery mentality" often prevails in societies where no opportunities for betterment can be seen. Parents cling to the hope that if they have enough children, perhaps one will be smart enough to get an education and free the family from poverty. While many children become an economic drain to parents earning adequate wages, when wages are too small to support the family, or the parents are unemployed, children can be an asset. They can support the family by working in the informal economy, performing such services as washing windshields or selling candy and trinkets in the streets (Lappe, *Population* 21-24). Although population growth has stabilized in the industrial nations, growth continues at an alarming rate in the world's poorer regions, adding further pressure to the crisis.

Heightened economic pressure in the Third World has also led to the problems of war and migration. Ever-increasing competition for scarce resources among local peoples in the world's undeveloped regions has ignited pre-existing rivalries into a steadily increasing number regional wars. Many of the newly formed nations in the Third World have had to contend with conflicts between various groups of heterogenous peoples who found themselves fenced in by arbitrary national borders drawn by the colonial powers of the previous era. It is not surprising, therefore, that 174 of the 186 wars since 1945 have occurred in the Third World (Hauchler and Kennedy, 179).

Refugees attempting to escape war or persecution from opposing groups in power now number about 16 million worldwide. To be added to these are between ten and twenty million more people who have been uprooted and live as refugees within their own countries. Others have attempted to escape the dire poverty at home by working illegally in First World nations. Currently, there are estimated to be 175 million illegal workers worldwide, eleven million of whom reside in the United States. Such workers are often exploited since they do not have the same rights as citizens and are willing to submit to many abuses for fear of deportation (Hauchler and Kennedy 124-126; Papademetriou).

As the undeveloped world sank further and further into poverty, America enjoyed a "wonderful moment" of prosperity during the 1990s and early 2000s. By the mid-1990s, the United States had experienced the greatest economic boom in 25 years and the third longest on record. GNP growth was steady at 2%. Unemployment dropped to under 5%, a 24-year low, while inflation hovered at approximately 3%. For years policymakers had been unsuccessful in their attempts to reduce joblessness without simultaneously increasing inflation. Central Bank Chairman Alan Greenspan was given the credit for achieving this miracle and dubbed "Maestro." (Baumohl 54).

With a spirit characteristic of every generation of those caught up in the euphoria of an economic boom, rational explanations were put forth to demonstrate why this one was different from all the rest: "Those decades came to ugly conclusions, alas, but this one is likely to be different. Why? Unlike most earlier expansions, which crashed to earth when the Federal Reserve raised interest rates sharply to cool down an over-inflating economy, the 1990s-style growth shows few signs of strain. To the contrary, a rare combination of price stability and moderate gains in the gross domestic product has made this upturn remarkably steady" (Pooley 32). America's "wonderful moment" was felt not only by the capitalist class, but by the public at large. A contemporary TIME/CNN poll indicated that 54% of Americans, nearly half of whom were earning less than $20,000 a year, felt like they were living in a period of "good times" for the country (Pooley 30). The perceptions of the people and the pundits of that era seem ridiculously naive to someone living in the post-apocalyptic world following the 2007 financial crisis.

Whether in good times or bad, peoples' perceptions must be manipulated to keep the party going as long as possible and to keep everyone from running for the doors once the fire breaks out. The mass media has become a highly effective tool for shaping the opinions and ideology of the public at large. Approximately 20 media companies print and distribute the majority of the materials read by the public. Local newspapers are almost always owned by larger corporations. Those desiring to express viewpoints divergent from corporate interests are faced with editors unwilling to publish articles that would threaten their corporate advertising constituency. The costs of independent publication or television airing have become prohibitive for any organization that does not have deep financial pockets. The Internet held the promise of leveling the playing field, but the era of free ranging on the frontier is quickly coming to a close. Most people surfing the Internet are now corralled into feed lots where they are provided with information supplied by the highest bidder to the search engines.

Convincing the public that the financial crisis is over and that they should spend rather than save has become paramount in the effort to keep resources flowing toward the top. Yet eventually, even those living in the Penthouse will have their day of reckoning, as there is no longer any structural basis for the prosperity that was enjoyed by so many in the decades following WWII. This fact is neglected in the many financial articles penned by hedge fund managers and big bank economists. They cite numerous statistics as indicators of a renewed growth spurt. They claim to see the forest from a distance, but they have not walked through it and looked at the state of the trees—or of the soil they are planted in, which has become depleted of the essential nutrients necessary to sustain growth.

Given the similarity between the patterns visible in the American systemic cycle of capital accumulation and those of the Genoese, Dutch, and British regimes, the most logical conclusion is that the U.S. position of hegemony over the world capitalist system is coming to a close, as signaled by the shift from investment in trade and production to high finance and the accompanying "wonderful moment" which this shift produced (and which now appears to have ended catastrophically). Nevertheless, since the 1970s the debate has raged on between "declinists" who prophesy America's fall and "revivalists" hopeful of a renewed cycle of US dominance over world markets (Hauchler and Kennedy 36). An obvious question for the revivalists is why, and more specifically—with what resources, such a return to dominance will come about. The answer provided by most seems to be, "Because we are Americans." The resources part of the question doesn't appear to be that relevant.

Chapter 2

Ken Lay and Executive Pay

In 1985 the Houston Natural Gas company and the Internorth company of Omaha, Nebraska merged their individual gas pipelines to form the first national supply grid. Shortly thereafter Ken Lay, the former CEO of Houston Natural Gas, became the CEO of the newly-named Enron Corporation. The company expanded rapidly, making a market by setting up contracts with businesses and utilities to deliver gas and oil at fixed prices on future dates. From the late 1980s through the late 1990s, Enron began a series of acquisitions of energy-related businesses around the world. In the United States the company profited from the deregulation of electrical power markets, gaining access to an industry that had previously been controlled by government entities. To facilitate its numerous deals brokering energy commodities, Enron began to weave a complex web of financial operations and political connections.

When annual revenues topped $100 billion and the stock price peaked at $84.87 in the year 2000, no one could have imagined what lay just around the corner. The heroic general who had led the company to such a stunning conquest, chief executive Ken Lay, rewarded himself handsomely, receiving $53 million in annual compensation with exercised stock options of more than $123 million and un-exercised (year 2000) options of more than $361 million. A number of his most trusted top officers shared in the spoils as well. Then the meltdown began. In October of 2001 the company reported a $638 million loss for the third quarter and a $1.2 billion reduction in shareholder equity. A formal investigation by the SEC subsequently uncovered a host of unethical dealings and fraudulent actions by Enron executives and consultants from the prestigious accounting firm Arthur Andersen. In addition to the more than 6100 employees who lost their jobs, health insurance, and retirement benefits with Enron's collapse, thousands of others watched their retirement funds disappear as the price of Enron stock sank into oblivion (AFL-CIO).

The Enron debacle provides a poignant reminder of the urgent need to establish enforceable measures of corporate social accountability. Such *accountability* should be distinguished from *responsibility*. Corporate responsibility, since it is voluntary, still remains largely an ideal. Corporate accountability, however, is certainly achievable. In light of the Enron scandal and others that have filled the news in recent years, it is incumbent upon socially responsible citizens to demand greater accountability from the corporate entities that exercise so much control over their lives and futures. Of the myriad acts of social injustice that have been committed by certain irresponsible corporations—from polluting the environment to knowingly marketing unsafe products—there is perhaps none that has been more readily tolerated than the practice of granting exorbitant amounts of compensation to corporate chieftains.

The practice has been justified by the delusion that highly talented CEOs deserve lavish pay packages because they add real value which can ultimately be reaped by the stockholders. Their huge monetary rewards are believed to be part and parcel with capitalism itself. Yet it is ultimately the stockholders (the true torchbearers of capitalism) who lose out, since the rewards of production are not distributed to them as dividends or reinvested in the company to add value to the shares they already own. In the case of Enron, pillage of the corporate treasury and the confiscation of shareholder value by granting enormous stock options ultimately weakened the company's infrastructure to the point of collapse. Such a scenario has often been played out in the political realm by Third World dictators who enrich themselves from public funds and sell off government assets when the coffers become empty, leaving the citizens with a bankrupt nation and a debt-service burden that will remain for years to come. Unlike corrupt dictators, who frequently suffer the consequences of their actions in the end, executives are rarely called to account unless they have been guilty of outright fraud, as in the case of Enron.

Although there are numerous examples of excessive executive pay in the annals of America's business history, a marked change began to take shape in the late 1980s. In 1980 the average CEO to hourly worker pay ratio was 42-to-1. This ratio rose to 85-to-1 in 1990 and now stands at 380-to-1 (AFL-CIO). One of the principle causes of this trend was the growing belief among institutional investors that the performance of a company was inextricably linked to the performance of its CEO. Prior to 1960 less than 10 percent of the stock in publicly-traded companies was owned by institutional investors, a number which has grown to more than 60 percent today. As more and more institutions and money managers began acquiring stock, they became increasingly interested in the performance of the companies that they held.

During the heyday of corporate takeovers in the early 1980s, institutional investors used their enormous resources to facilitate leveraged buyouts and oust underperforming CEOs. Within a few years state governments began to frustrate these efforts by enacting anti-takeover laws. By this time the "personalization" of company performance in the figure of a superstar CEO had already become well established. With their ability to take over companies and oust under-performing CEOs severely limited, institutional investors began to put pressure on boards of directors to carry out this task for them. In order to entice corporate superstars to come over and take the helm, boards of directors began to offer larger and larger incentive packages, a process that has been spiraling upward ever since (Conan). Although many institutional investors now loath the monster that they helped to create, others in the money management business prefer not to rock the boat for fear of a backlash against their own exorbitant salaries.

At the height of the internet boom executive compensation packages reached truly astronomical levels. The average CEO paycheck in 1999 ($12.4 million) was more than six times the average CEO paycheck in 1990. The top five CEOs in a list compiled by *BusinessWeek* earned a cumulative $1.2 billion in 1999; and the top 20 CEOs averaged $112.9 million each (Reingold). Pay packages tapered off somewhat following the Internet bust, but many CEOs still received compensation packages worth tens of millions of dollars.

The 2007 financial crisis finally gave these corporate prima donnas their first real haircut. Then the Dodd-Frank Wall Street Reform and Consumer Protection Act kicked in 2010, requiring companies to ask shareholders for approval of executive pay packages. Unfortunately, the approval is non-binding, a loophole that allows the greediest CEOs to make off with more than their fair share of booty. Lawrence Ellison of Oracle was paid $96 million in 2012, even though less than half of the company's shareholders approved this amount. (Schwartz).

Compensation for chief executives can take a variety of forms. At the most basic level are salaries, which are benchmarked according to general industry surveys that report pay percentiles based on company size. Size is typically determined by revenues or market capitalization. These surveys fail to incorporate such relevant factors as age, education, and experience—items which must be built into various adjustments made by compensation committees. A typical contract will guarantee increases in base salary levels for the next five years. Most companies also offer annual bonus plans based on the performance for the year. A typical bonus plan provides a minimum bonus once a certain threshold of performance has been reached. Rewards then increase incrementally until reaching a cap. Although some companies include certain non-financial performance measures, most rely upon a percentage based on annual profits.

The stock option is another type of compensation that has become increasingly popular in recent years. Stock options allow CEOs to buy shares of the company's stock at a specified "exercise" price for a certain time period. Most options are valid for up to ten years and are exercisable at the fair market value at the time they are granted. Some firms issue "discount options" at prices below the fair market value of the stock, while others issue "premium options" at prices above the fair market value. The rationale behind stock options is that executives will be rewarded commensurate with appreciation of the company's outstanding shares. If share price declines options are sometimes re-priced at a lower value to maintain their incentive for the CEO. Thus, unlike the typical shareholder, many executives are to a certain degree insured against loss. In contrast to the traditional maritime code of honor, it is the passengers that go down with the ship while the captain and officers get into the lifeboats. One of the reasons stock options have become so popular is that they are, for the most part, invisible in the corporate financial statements, since the granting of an option does not constitute a taxable event either for the company or the executive until they are exercised.

Another important component of executive pay is the retirement plan. Most CEOs of major corporations enjoy *Supplemental Executive Retirement Plans (SERPS)* in addition to the regular retirement plans provided to other members of the company. SERPS constitute one of the most elusive forms of executive pay for those desiring to pin down the total value of a compensation package. Payments to SERPS are typically not disclosed in public financial statements, since retired executives are no longer company employees (Murphy, 9-24). When Jack Welch stepped down as CEO of General Electric, he received a Manhattan apartment and continued use of the corporate jet as part of his retirement package. These fringe benefits amounted to nearly $2.5 million in value and only became publicly known because of a mandatory disclosure for Welch's divorce hearing (Fonda, 63).

The natural question that emerges after surveying the typical CEO incentive package is: How do all of these financial motivators affect performance? Before this question can be answered, it is necessary to determine how performance is to be measured. Increasing stock price is a very inaccurate gauge, since bull markets tend to buoy up the majority of Fortune 500 companies. "When the tide comes in all the ships rise." Although a few of these "ships" may fail to maintain the integrity of their hulls and end up sinking, most will have enough strength in their ongoing business operations and market share to make it difficult to isolate the effect of the CEO. Academic studies of the effect of CEOs on company performance have generated mixed results (Murphy, 26-43). On a more intuitive level, it seems absurd to attribute so much value to the talents of a few individuals while ignoring the aggregate contribution of the numerous skilled employees that ultimately make a company function. Often the specific technical skills that are the lifeblood of a company are rewarded with a mere pittance in comparison to the rewards top executives receive for their charisma and supposed ability to see "the big picture."

Researchers in the field of Organizational Behavior (OB) have analyzed the effects of *organizational justice*—the sense of fairness people have about their treatment within an organization—on their job performance. Organizational justice has a number of forms, one of which has been termed *distributive justice*. Distributive justice refers to the perception people have about how fairly they are being compensated for their efforts within an organization. In a perfect world of unlimited resources employees might not be bothered by a huge disparity between their pay share and that of the top executives. However, since resources within any given organization are limited, it is unlikely that a company could have the means to pay every employee a large salary that would meet all of his or her needs. To the extent that everyone is compensated fairly and salary differences are pegged to readily identifiable skill levels, experience, or longevity at the company, such differences will be tolerated. Yet when such large multiples exist between the salaries of ground level employees and those at the top, workers will begin to sense distributive injustice and lose motivation. Ultimately performance will suffer (Greenberg, 38).

Equity Theory elaborates on the concept of distributive justice and describes the ways people respond to it. According to equity theory, people compare themselves to others on the basis of outcomes and inputs. When they perceive that someone else has a higher outcome/input ratio than they do, they feel angry and resentful and seek to create a greater state of equity. This may be accomplished by lowering inputs—slacking off on the job, calling in sick more often, or even quitting; or, by attempting to increase outcomes—stealing company property, etc. Although the effects predicted by equity theory are strongest when an employee compares himself to a highly visible coworker, the relative distance and invisibility of the CEO to the average ground-level employee is no safeguard. At some point higher up the ladder an employee will sense inequity when making comparisons with an immediate superior. To the extent that such differences seem reasonable based on job position they will be tolerated. Yet if the disparity is too large a sense of injustice will set in. If an unjustly paid executive attempts to co-opt his immediate subordinate through inclusion in the high pay "club," the sense of inequity will only be passed one more rung down the ladder—not eliminated (Greenberg, 192-194).

America, like so many other nations, is witnessing a gradual erosion of its middle class. Lower taxes and shrinking government services have the ultimate effect of reducing the income of the country's poorest citizens, since their taxes are already at a minimum and needed services such as healthcare, food and housing take a huge bite out of their total income. As the ranks of the nations' poor grow larger, the wealth of the country's richest citizens is reaching unprecedented levels. Those in the middle, once the backbone of America, are finding it increasingly difficult to hold on to their current position. As one might expect, the tendency is to slide downward rather than upward. Solid, middle-class jobs with a good wage, retirement benefits and health insurance are more and more difficult to find. Even when such jobs can be found, peoples' hold on them is tenuous at best. Many corporations prefer to hire temporary workers so that they are not bound to pay for their health insurance or retirement benefits.

In some ways the world has not changed much over the millennia. Even the ancient Romans often granted slaves their freedom at around age 30 (considered old age back then) so that they would no longer be a liability. In an era of such booming prosperity for American business it is hard to imagine that the country's largest corporations are too strapped to provide good wages and benefits for their employees. The fact is that a disproportionate amount of the harvest of America's productivity is being reaped by corporate overlords while the workers are left to glean the fields. Once a precedent has been set for greed, more and more people want to get in on the action. The companies that do choose to act responsibly and place reasonable limits on executive pay face strong pressure to conform to the culturally accepted norms or risk losing talented executives.

The greed which powers the capitalist system, like uranium, can unleash tremendous productive energy. But unless it is regulated by some social equivalent of a cadmium rod, it will burn out of control and destroy the lives of the people that it is supposed to benefit. Corporations are simply not capable of policing themselves. In the absence of responsibility there must be accountability. An external authority with sufficient power, i.e., the government, is needed to regulate the entities on which its citizens depend for their well-being.

For many, the idea of greater government involvement in business affairs seems like an anathema. However, the problem of excessive executive pay could be solved in a relatively simple way with minimal governmental intervention by using one of its most powerful and effective tools—taxation. If executives opt to receive an exorbitant amount of pay instead of plowing those funds back into the company infrastructure (including both its human and material resources), the government could step in and tax away the executive's windfall, plowing it back into society in some way.

The ranks of America's workers will certainly benefit from such a change, but ultimately the stockholders (who may also include those workers) will reap the greatest rewards. Reinvesting profits back into whole companies (instead of into a few individuals) will add greater value and equip America's industries to compete more effectively in the global marketplace, thereby increasing the value of the outstanding shares of stock. Perhaps in the short-run using company profits or equity to hire a superstar may drive up the stock price, but such a system is not sustainable.

Chapter 3

Corporate Morlocks

In his book *The Time Machine* the British author H.G. Wells tells the story of an inventor who builds a time machine and travels thousands of years into the future. When the inventor arrives at his destination, he finds a strange society of gentle, peaceful, and unusually happy people inhabiting the land that was once Industrial Age England. The people lead carefree lives, residing in beautiful marble buildings and eating only fruits and vegetables, which are mysteriously provided for them each day. The young inventor is at first taken in by this apparent utopia of the future, but eventually he becomes curious about how it functions. He discovers a number of round openings in the ground that lead to a vast underground network of tunnels. When he explores one of the passages, he finds that the subterranean level of this utopia is inhabited by a carnivorous race of beings called Morlocks, who control the machinery and technology that sustains the people above the ground. The Morlocks allow the people to live a blissful existence and provide for all of their needs, but each night they crawl out of the tunnels and drag some of them underground to eat them.

If H.G. Wells' time machine had stopped in early 21st century America, the rudimentary pattern for the future world he envisioned would already be evident. Everything people need seems to be magically provided for them—plenty of greasy fast food (a fruit and vegetable diet is still a long way off), electronic gadgets, and cheap clothing. Bigger toys like cars and TV sets can be obtained with easily available credit. Yet if one dares to look beneath the surface, he will find a race of elites who control the machinery and technology that makes this society possible. These "corporate Morlocks" prey on a clueless class of consumers who have no idea how the whole system works. They borrow and spend with blissful abandon, not realizing that their destiny is to be eaten up by their debt to the Morlocks. Escape is impossible—unless you have a time machine that can take you back to an era when people worked hard and made due with less, and saved their money instead of spending it.

# Chapter 4

GDP and Me

Gross Domestic Product (GDP) is the total value of all the goods and services a country produces. When this number is divided by the total number of people living in a country, you get the *Per Capita Income*. Thus, countries with people who are making a lot of stuff or doing things that they can charge a good price for will have a larger GDP—and will usually be richer. But if there are a lot of people who either aren't working or working at low paying jobs, the country's GDP will be lower. This is why even a large country like China had a relatively low GDP and remained poor during much of the 20th Century. Its people just weren't producing a lot of high value goods and services. Most of them worked as unskilled laborers or subsistence farmers. The United States, on the other hand, enjoyed a very high GDP during much of the 20th Century. In the year 1950, Americans, representing only 6% of the world's population, produced 27% of world GDP. Western Europe, with 12% of the world's population, produced 26% of world GDP; India, with 14% of the world's population, produced 14% of world GDP; China, with 22% of the world's population, produced 4% of world GDP; and Japan, with 3% of the world's population, produced 3% of world GDP (Taylor 2008).

Thus, in those days America was making a lot of money to divvy up among its citizens. The average worker's cut was about one fortieth that of the bosses running the corporations that were fueling much of the country's economic growth. By the mid-1950s, the unemployment rate had dropped to less than 3%, so most people had a job.

Surprisingly, the United States still produces about 25% of world GDP, but a lot has changed. CEOs now make about 380 times what the average worker makes. Even an artificially low unemployment rate of 9%, which doesn't include people who have quit looking for jobs, means that millions of people are not receiving a share of the proceeds from the nation's aggregate economic activity. The widespread practice of shipping manufacturing jobs overseas has preserved corporate profits (and in the process maintained previous levels of economic output reflected in GDP), but resulted in a declining middle class. Displaced workers are forced to accept low-paying jobs in the service sector—i.e, becoming Walmart "Associates" or flipping burgers at McDonalds. In other words, they have become poor, often without even realizing it. The illusion of a middle class existence is maintained by a plethora of material goods that their parents and grandparents never had back in the 1950s.

These devices are often purchased on credit with high rates of interest. A massive industry has emerged to provide financing to poor people for everything from cheaply made houses, to cars, to electronic gadgets. All of this lending and spending also gets included in the GDP—the total amount of goods and services that the country produces—accounting for 70% of it. Meanwhile China, now responsible for 9.5% of world GDP, generates an ever growing income for its citizens by manufacturing and selling most of the items that the indebted Americans keep buying. China's GDP growth has averaged 10% per year over the past 30 years. America's GDP growth has averaged less than 3% during the same period, and the ongoing financial crisis does not bode well for the future. The massive amount of personal debt means that people are eventually going to have to stop buying stuff other than absolute necessities. The massive amount of government debt means that Washington can't take up the slack by hiring lots of people to do things other than the basics that are required to keep the nation running. So, GDP will inevitably decrease—and people will inevitably become poorer than they once were.

So what does this have to do with me? Well, you might fare better than the Joneses down the street, but we're all in the same ship together. It would be nice if any one of us could set things right and put the nation back on the proper heading, but we will always be limited as individuals. What you can do, though, is start making preparations now for the lean years ahead. This will be far more beneficial than spending like a drunken sailor in the vain hope that it's all going to get better soon. Policymakers realize that the quickest and easiest way to stave off the inevitable—and hang on to their government paychecks as long as possible—will be to encourage people to keep spending, even if they have to take on more debt to do so. But this course of action will be bad for you and ultimately bad for the country. It is amazing to hear and read about people who are going out and buying things, thinking they are fulfilling some sort of patriotic duty. It's time to stop drinking the Kool Aid constantly being poured out by the media and start doing what common sense should make obvious. Save everything you can, invest in yourself to develop marketable skills that will enable you to effectively compete in a ruthless job market, then save some more money and develop some more skills.

Chapter 5

Nation Slaves

A popular self-deprecating joke among Brazilians tells the story of how one of the angels in heaven questions God during the creation of the world and asks, "Why are you creating such a vast, beautiful territory with abundant water, fertile soil, timber, minerals, and other natural resources and no earthquakes, tornados, or hurricanes? It won't be fair to the other countries!" God responds with a smile and says, "Don't worry. Just wait 'til you see the people I'm going to put there!" The joke betrays the Brazilians' acknowledgement of living in such an ironic condition—even in a large country with abundant resources, poverty abounds. Less to blame than the people, however, is the system in which they live—a global economic system that has resulted in a similar irony throughout the world. Even in the United States, the world's richest nation, 39.3 million people live below the official government poverty line. But poor Americans, especially poor American children, still have it pretty good compared to the Brazilians.

Born into displaced rural families that have settled on the fringes of the city in the hope of finding work, many of Brazil's poor children end up being exploited as prostitutes or couriers in the drug trade. They are a cheap, replaceable source of labor for adults. Those that remain independent survive by committing petty street crimes. The numerous small shopkeepers, frustrated with an ineffective police system, turn to private "death squads" to rid the streets of these "vermin" and protect their goods. The general public, worried about personal security, is usually supportive of the measures taken to reduce the threat from these little terrors.

Displaced families, street children, and crime are

some of the more obvious social ills that are becoming more and more common throughout the world in the present era of turbo-capitalism. Less obvious to the general public are the oppressive sweatshops located in the free trade zones of the Third World, as well as in the inner cities of the United States. Young women, thanks to their docile nature, manual dexterity, and willingness to do boring, repetitive work, have become the preferred labor commodity of the transnational corporations searching for cheap labor with no government regulations.

Powerful organizations, such as UNIDO, the IMF, and the World Bank, require Third World countries needing loans to conform to the economic blueprint devised by the leading industrial nations. The policies implemented, such as the elimination of import tariffs, tax breaks for foreign investors, and the creation of free trade zones, convert poorer nations from self-sustaining agricultural economies to "export platforms" servicing the more powerful nations. These poorer countries become in effect "nation-slaves" to their industrial masters. Thus, the ancient practice of debt-ridden individuals being sold into slavery is now being reproduced at a national scale, with the accompanying oppression and suffering being passed on directly to the citizens. Yet the First World masters should not be quick to relish in their more fortunate position. As many individuals have had to learn, "What goes around comes around."

Chapter 6

The Politics of Persuasion

Those who travel along the roads of South Florida are very familiar with the vast network of canals that drain the water of the Everglades into the ocean. These canals also provide an inexpensive form of recreation and meals for some of the community's "less fortunate" people, who can frequently be seen on the banks fishing for small brim and catfish. Those who are a bit more prosperous are able to purchase small boats and gain access to various wildlife preserves within the Everglades itself and catch largemouth bass, which provide considerably more entertainment than the smaller fish that pass through the locks into the canals. They are also more fortunate in that they are able to see the large warning signs posted near the boat ramps informing them of the danger of eating more than one phosphorus and mercury fortified fish per week from the contaminated waters.

Environmentalists have fought for years to implement government regulations which would require the large, family-owned sugar plantations to clean up these waters that their government-subsidized operations have polluted. After years of fighting against the powerful lobbying of the sugar barons, those who wanted to protect these unique wetlands for posterity were finally able to take the issue to the public by placing on the 1996 election ballot a proposal for a 1% tax on sugar to be used to clean up the Everglades. The sugar industry responded with a massive $30,000,000 media campaign to shape public opinion in their favor before the vote took place. The airwaves were deluged with ads urging people to vote against the tax. The ads made no reference to anything of substance or logic but rather spoke of vague generalities that reflected popular sentiments, such as "don't let the government add any new taxes" and "the government has mismanaged millions of dollars of taxpayers money—don't let them do it again by giving them more." Amazingly, the public was persuaded to vote against their own interests in favor of the private interests of the sugar industry. Tactics similar to these have been utilized by the private sector over the past few decades to win citizen support for policies which in reality cheat the public and benefit big business and the wealthy.

The programs of Roosevelt's New Deal and Johnson's War on Poverty ushered in badly needed social reforms and gave birth to the protective agencies that would work to ameliorate the suffering of those who didn't end up benefitting from the capitalist system. The idea gradually began to take hold that the government had the responsibility of preventing and relieving the suffering of its citizens. In spite of its limitations, the War on Poverty, along with the reforms of the Kennedy era, resulted in the poverty rate being cut in half between 1960 and 1972. Nevertheless, the progress would be short-lived.

Big-business, longing for the glory days of unfettered capitalism and pressured by the increased competition of the emerging global economy, began to marshal its forces to take back the lost ground. Taking advantage of the eroding public trust of government after Viet Nam and Watergate, a rallying cry against big government and the corrupt welfare state was sent out through the "new and refurbished foundations, legal organizations, opinion journals, newspapers, radio and television programs, and think tanks, funded by ultra-conservative corporate interests" (Collins, p.108). By propagating statements about "welfare queens" and "fat bureaucrats," big business was able to convince the middle-class to vote in officials who would use their influence to reverse the reforms of the past and legislate policies which would favor corporations and the wealthy. In view of these developments it is more important than ever for people to educate themselves rather than simply entrusting this task to the mass media.

Chapter 7

The Welfare State

Nearly 3500 years ago Moses led a large group of former slaves out of Egypt and into the land of Palestine to form a nation of their own. As slaves they had all been equal and had shared a common experience of oppression and poverty. Upon entering the new territory, they would establish a simple agrarian society held together by the bonds of a clan structure and a common religion. At the core of their religion was a set of laws governing the moral and civic responsibilities of the citizens of this nation-to-be. A portion of these laws were contained in the well-known "Ten Commandments." Yet there were a number of other laws as well, some of which dealt with the issue of poverty. One such law states "There will always be poor people in the land. Therefore I command you to be open-handed towards your brothers and towards the poor and needy in your land (Deuteronomy 15:11)." About 750 years later, one of the Israelite prophets made an assessment of how well they had put this law into practice: "You trample on the poor and force him to give you grain. Therefore, though you have built stone mansions, you will not live in them; though you have planted lush vineyards you will not drink their wine (Amos 5:11)." This early "Welfare State" failed because the citizens were unwilling to yield to even the "Highest Authority."

More than 200 years ago a group of settlers who had left Europe for America declared their independence from Britain and formed a nation of their own. They were a simple, agrarian society held together by a somewhat common religion and a common cultural heritage. At the core of their religion was the *Protestant Work Ethic*, a moral and ethical system that stressed economic success.

Emanating from the ideas of John Calvin, this system stressed the belief that only a few people were chosen for salvation. People were urged to work hard to attain the prosperity that would be seen as a sign that they were among the chosen few. This view bolstered capitalism and legitimized an unequal stratification system in the new nation by generating the idea that poverty was a divine punishment for the damned.

With the Protestant Work Ethic at the heart of the values of the new nation, it is no wonder that governmental reforms on behalf of the poor have faced a constant battle in the United States. The first major attack on public aid occurred in the 1820s, when a growing landless population began to settle in the cities and suffered from low wages and irregular work. City officials responded by auctioning them off to the highest bidder, contracting them out to local farmers, and even barring indigents in need of relief from settling in their towns. In 1824 poor law reforms were made that replaced "outdoor" or "home" relief with an "indoor" relief system of workhouses and poorhouses. These institutions quickly deteriorated into degrading warehouses where the poor were crammed in along with criminals, the physically ill, and the insane.

During the latter part of the 19th century the policy of separating children from their families in order "to break the line of pauper descent" was widely followed. The Mother's Pension program improved the lives of some "deserving widows," but it also perpetuated the charity model of public assistance: low benefits, sporadic implementation, and emphasis on moral reform. This program was incorporated into the 1935 Social Security

Act as Aid to Dependent Children, which was to become Aid to Families with Dependent Children after the 1962 Social Security Act amendments. This is the program that has become the scapegoat for the current attacks on welfare.

Over the past 200 years the face of relief for the poor has changed according to the prevailing norms and methodologies of the day. What has not changed are the underlying structural constraints of the Protestant Work Ethic and the competing demand for women's unpaid labor in the home and their low-paid labor in the market. Unfortunately, the "Highest Authority" seems to be the dollar, to which far too many citizens have so far been willing to yield.

Chapter 8

The New Sparta

Around the year 600 B.C. the alliance of Greek city states called Sparta enacted a series of radical political reforms that transformed the nation into a military society. All boys were required to begin military drills at the age of 7. Men were permitted to marry at the age of 20, but were required to live in the barracks until the age of 30. All men were required to eat at the public mess. One can readily imagine what family life must have been like in such a community. The burden of maintaining the home and raising the young children fell solely on the mother. Although the idea of such a cold, austere, and robot-like existence seems revolting to modern Americans, there are in fact many similarities between our society and that of ancient Sparta.

Few would deny that the ideal *"Leave It To Beaver"* family of the 1950s has largely disappeared. In 1970, approximately 11 percent of families were maintained by women alone (no husband present); by 1988, this percentage had more than doubled. Now, one in four American children are raised by a single parent, usually a woman (Amott, Armario). In order to support themselves and their children a growing number of women have had to enter the workforce, usually taking on the jobs that men do not want because of low pay and lack of benefits. Once they leave their jobs they come home to begin their "second shift" of unpaid housework and childcare. Although women are expected to diligently perform their role of *social reproduction* (reproducing society by maintaining the current generation and raising the next) their ability to do so is being exposed to increasing constraints as their real wages and benefits decrease and access to government aid programs, such as AFDC, is curtailed. As women work longer hours and second or third jobs in order to make ends meet, their ability to turn the home into an affective site, where children are nurtured and taught, is increasingly diminished. Instead of being raised by parents that provide them with love, security, and affection, children are instead raised by underpaid and disillusioned proxies at daycare centers. When they finally do get to spend some time with their natural mother at the end of the day she is exhausted from work and pressured to get needed housework done. If the father even lives in the home he usually doesn't return until late, having already eaten at the drive-thru "public mess."

Fortunately, young boys are still not required by the state to perform military drills at the age of 7. Nevertheless, local gangs have more than made up for this absence. In the hood young boys are required, sometimes at an age younger than 7, to give their allegiance to a local gang and participate in frequent skirmishes with rivals. The gangs fill the need for a sense of belonging and purpose which the family has failed to provide.

Sparta, despite it's powerful army and preeminent position after the Peloponnesian War, failed to produce a society which would leave a cultural legacy for the rest of the world—this would be accomplished by Athens. The United States, despite the most powerful army in the world and preeminent position after World War II, must be careful to take the necessary measures to build the kind of society that will flourish for many generations to come and leave a cultural legacy for the future.

Chapter 9

The Golden Rule

The Golden Rule has been rephrased popularly into the humorous cliche, "He who has the gold makes the rules." This principle, though perhaps not stated so succinctly, has been discussed by the greatest philosophers, debated in the courtrooms, ruling councils, senates, and parliaments throughout the ages, and proclaimed by great revolutionary leaders to establish new nations. Those who have attempted to abolish this principle have at the most only hidden it temporarily, as in the case of the housewife who makes a futile attempt to destroy the cockroaches in her home by turning on the lights and whacking them with the broom, only to find them again night after night. Of course, someone else can take the gold from the one making the rules and make different rules, as the Angles and Saxons took it from the Romans, the Normans took it from the Angles and Saxons, the Americans took it from the British, the Spanish took it from the Aztecs, or the Bolsheviks took it from the Czar. But no matter who ends up with the gold (economic capital), they will make the rules which will inevitably favor themselves.

Thus it should come as no surprise that even in a great democracy such as the United States "those with the most wealth ultimately have the most to say about politics most of the time—especially about those policies that affect economic life" (Collins, p.26). Nowhere is this principle more evident than in the U.S. tax code, which has in fact become two distinct tax systems, one for the privileged person and one for the common person.

Perhaps the cockroaches ran under the refrigerator during the 1950s and early 1960s, but it was inevitable that they would return. Why is this the case?

For one thing, it is part of human nature to act with self-interest. This is evident with children, with a husband and wife, with a team, a business, or a government. However noble and self-sacrificing a person may be—and there have been a number of such individuals throughout history—the norm is to act with self-interest. Certainly the founding fathers of the United States, enamoured as they were with the Enlightenment's elevated views of mankind, astutely recognized the need to create a government balanced between the powers of the executive, legislative, and judiciary branches in order to prevent an authoritarian takeover. They succeeded quite well in this, yet they failed to devise a system to prevent the rise of an oligarchy—perhaps because they *were* an oligarchy! Now, more than two hundred years later, social and economic inequality persists.

The myth of the middle class is perpetuated by the small but powerful group of people who control the mass media while the tax laws that favor the rich steadily eat away at the ranks of this supposed "backbone" of America. The laws are made so complex that even the wealthy can't understand them, but instead pay hefty fees to accountants and lawyers who then ensure that the progressive rate structure will not cause the majority of the tax burden to fall on them. Those in the highest income bracket often pay at a rate lower than those in lower brackets and in some cases don't pay any taxes at all. The accountants and lawyers who service the wealthy and are aware of the many loopholes would certainly not "bite the hand that feeds them" by trying to change things. Besides, in time they themselves might even be able to cross over into the ranks of the wealthy. The Tax

Reform Acts of 1969, 1976, and 1986 all claimed to plug the loopholes and shift more of the tax burden to the wealthy. Perhaps what's left of the middle class should more loudly voice the phrase which Tom Cruise shouted out in the movie *Jerry Mcguire,* "Show me the money!"

Chapter 10

Rat-proofing Your Portfolio

When early human beings lived as hunter-gatherers, they were unable to store much of the surplus from their productive labor. Most of what they produced was consumed or carried around on their backs. Everything changed once people started settling down and farming. Now they could produce so much food that a good portion of it could be set aside for the winter months. The big challenge, however, was storing it so that it could be protected from an ubiquitous and relentless enemy—the rat. Fortunately, our ancestors developed an amazing technology that solved this problem—pottery. As long as the food remained sealed up inside of hard, earthenware containers, the rats couldn't get to it.

We've come a long way since those early days. If the rats get into our pantry we just buy some new food and call Orkin. Yet, as with many aspects of our history, some things change and other things stay the same. There are still plenty of rats around that can get into our surpluses. If you live in a modern, industrialized nation you don't typically store all the bounty from your labor in the form of a big hoard of grain. Prudent people who don't consume all of their earnings in living expenses typically set aside their surpluses in the form of financial instruments—savings accounts, bonds, or stocks. And once again, the problem arises of how to protect these instruments from an ubiquitous and relentless enemy—the rats of the financial world.

The most brazen among them will simply try to steal your savings by luring you into some type of Ponzi scheme or other financial scam. Yet others are much more subtle. They will simply feed off of your funds by charging management fees that will stifle your portfolio's growth and gradually erode its value. Even large, respected financial institutions are infested with such rats, who typically work under the direction of a "big cheese" at the top who gets a large cut of everyone's take. In a surprising reversal of roles, the rats now bait the traps for the people, convincing them to bring in all of their savings and put it into the hands of "professionals" who will do a better job managing it for them. This idea has been so relentlessly promoted by the financial industry that they have succeeded in convincing large numbers of smart, successful people that trying to make investment decisions on their own is pure foolhardiness.

One of the industry's most effective tactics has been to confuse people by constantly spinning out an ever-changing array of complex financial products. Since people are busy earning their livelihoods, they don't have time to delve into the prospectuses of these offerings and decipher all of the arcane jargon. Many can be convinced that they need a professional to do this work for them. Little do they know that it is all a lot of crap and that even the professionals they deal with don't understand it either. They spend their days schmoozing clients on the phone, or in lunch appointments and golf games with the really rich ones in order to solidify the relationship. Supposedly, the analysts in the back room have a handle on things.

If clients have made bad investment decisions in the past, financial professionals can play on their insecurity, making them feel like they are not competent to manage their own money. Like children, they must hand it over to their parents so they won't lose it all. Surprisingly, many people are willing to let the experts demean them in this way.

More confident clients will not so easily acknowledge that the financial professionals are smarter than they are. They may start asking a lot of questions in their quest to understand the logic behind the complex financial products being pitched to them. These individuals must be gently steered away from the big secret in the back room—the big pile of rat @#%$. A very effective ploy is to stroke their egos, telling them that they are highly successful people and that they should spend their time doing what they do best while allowing others to take care of the tedious grunt work of managing finances. The appeal to a client's sense of self-importance is often powerful enough to cause him to abandon the quest for understanding and move on to greater things, leaving the management of finances to the "little people" that work for him. If all else fails, the rats can appeal to peoples' greed. Baiting the trap with promises of high returns is often overpowering, especially when a client is told that others are cashing in on this wonderful bounty while he is missing out because he is overly conservative.

Sadly, it appears that the rats will always be with us, evolving and adapting to our sophisticated economy where surpluses are stored in the form of intangible financial instruments rather than food supplies. Nevertheless, we can still protect ourselves using measures that are almost as simple and straightforward as putting grain in earthenware jars: *Keep your surpluses close at hand (not out in the barn), and seal them off from from financial professionals.* In other words, never, never relinquish the management of your portfolio to a professional at some hedge fund or financial institution. Even if you know nothing about investments and simply put everything into a savings account or bank CD to begin with, that's OK. Sure, you can do much better, and yes, inflation will be gradually decreasing the value of your savings with the low interest rates that banks offer. But you are not foolish to start out here. If you don't feel competent to buy stocks or bonds on your own, how could you possibly feel competent to properly judge the honesty and skill of someone who claims he can do it for you? Will you base your decision on his or her nice personality or recommendations from others who based their decision on his or her nice personality? Why not keep everything in the savings account at first and then do some reading and Internet research. Once you are confident, you can move everything over to an index fund or bond fund at a large, well-established investment firm.

Unless you have a brain injury or a severe mental illness, you can manage your own investments. And it's OK to move up the learning curve slowly, missing out on the higher returns that will come later once you are more proficient. Imagine if everyone had the attitude that driving an automobile was very complicated (which it is) and decided to pay a chauffeur to drive them around! You will certainly become a much better driver after doing it for many years, but not if you refuse to get behind the wheel in the first place.

Most of us will probably opt for the services of an accountant to prepare our tax returns every year. Unless they are employed by the Mob or Enron, most accountants do honorable work and can be relied upon to help us with tax planning and preparing our tax returns. In recent years, financial planners have become more popular, offering a more comprehensive service that includes such things as retirement planning, insurance, etc. If you choose to utilize their services, watch out! You'll need to know how to smell a rat. There are certainly some honest financial planners out there who will do a good job, but there are others who would love to get their greedy little paws on your portfolio and "manage" it for you for an annual percentage of the total value of the assets.

This sort of fee arrangement, though commonly accepted in the industry, makes no sense. Some may want to charge as much as 2%. This means that a retiree with a $100,000 portfolio will pay $2000 per year. Assuming that the manager successfully generates a 5% return on the assets (extremely difficult in today's market), and assuming a 3% inflation rate (extremely optimistic), you will effectively have earned 0% on your money. But that doesn't include taxes, so in effect you will be paying someone every year to lose money for you. If you are wealthy and hand over $10 million for the person to manage, you will pay $200,000 every year for the service. The average salary for a full professor at Harvard University is $192,600 (Jaschik). So, if you had $10 million to invest, for the amount of money you would pay a money manager, you could hire a Harvard finance professor to work full-time doing nothing but managing your (and only your) investment portfolio. He would be at your beckon and call every day whenever you wanted a snapshot of the latest economic news and academic research and how it pertained to your particular investments. This would certainly be a better value than the periodic lunch or golf game and schmoozing over the telephone. Since no money manager ever gives his clients such personalized attention, why should it cost so much more to manage a larger portfolio. One logical answer might be that for the higher fee you get to invest in the good stuff, whereas the small-time investor has to invest in the crap. But it doesn't work like airline seats or concert tickets, where the drastically-improved experience may justify the much higher price. The quality and diversity of the investments should be the same—you can just buy more of them with more money.

So what, pray tell, is the difference? Perhaps it is the added complexity involved with a larger portfolio. What complexity? As already mentioned, the investment mix and quality should be the same. Maybe it's the added burden of responsibility. Losing the millions entrusted by a wealthy person would be far more tragic than losing some small-time retiree's $100,000 portfolio. Would it?

If a financial planner is being compensated for the hours he or she must spend applying knowledge and skill to solving certain problems, it makes sense to compensate such a person based upon the time that is spent. Those with more extensive knowledge and skill would certainly be justified in charging a higher hourly rate. Nevertheless, the rate should be the same for everyone. Is it fair for a plumber to charge $200 per hour to fix a pipe in a large, expensive home and $60 per hour to fix the same pipe in a more humble dwelling? No, but of course, plumbers and and other home repair professionals are notorious for this sort of thing. Rating services such as Angie's List have now made it easier to avoid getting ripped off.

In the financial planning world, organizations such as The National Association of Personal Financial Advisors (NAPFA) have made an important effort to weed out advisors who receive kickbacks and bonuses by promoting certain products to their clients. This is an important step, but it is not enough. Those with larger portfolios will still end up paying exorbitantly high fees if they get suckered into some type of percentage based compensation arrangement. Prudent savers will steer clear of financial advisors who offer anything but a strict hourly fee-based compensation model.

Chapter 11

The Sausage Factory

Many years ago some hungry but enterprising individual decided that instead of mixing up another batch of dog food, he would grind up all those guts and other animal parts lying around the butcher shop floor, throw in some salt and other spices, and create a tasty new food product. Sausage was born. When meat production was scaled up during the Industrial Revolution, slaughterhouses were able to make enormous profits just by cleaning up all the leftover mess and throwing it into the hoppers. For many years, the details of what went on in these meat factories remained relatively secret. But in 1904, a young writer decided to go undercover and get a job at one of Chicago's meatpacking plants. He told the world about what he saw in his famous book, *The Jungle*:

> There was never the least attention paid to what was cut up for sausage; there would come all the way back from Europe old sausage that had been rejected, and that was moldy and white—it would be dosed with borax and glycerine, and dumped into the hoppers, and made over again for home consumption. There would be meat that had tumbled out on the floor, in the dirt and sawdust, where the workers had tramped and spit uncounted billions of consumption germs. There would be meat stored in great piles in rooms; and the water from leaky roofs would drip over it, and thousands of rats would race about on it. It was too dark in these storage places to see well, but a man could run his hand over these piles of meat and sweep off handfuls of the dried dung of rats. These rats were nuisances, and the packers would put

poisoned bread out for them; they would die, and then rats, bread, and meat would go into the hoppers together. This is no fairy story and no joke; the meat would be shoveled into carts, and the man who did the shoveling would not trouble to lift out a rat even when he saw one— there were things that went into the sausage in comparison with which a poisoned rat was a tidbit. (Sinclair 14:5).

President Theodore Roosevelt was so shaken up by what he read that he launched a government investigation, then established the USDA to police America's meat industry. For the most part, this government agency has been fairly effective at preventing the abuses that were once a common practice.

The SEC, charged with policing the financial industry, has had a much more difficult time of things. Foul financial instruments, though they abound in the warehouses of Wall Street, don't always give off a readily recognizable stench like rotten meat. Routine inspections often fail to spot a lot of the underlying filth. Fortunately, there are whistle-blowers who from time to time come forward and report what is really going on behind the scenes.

On March 14, 2012 Greg Smith, a high-ranking director at Goldman Sachs, shocked the financial world by publishing an exposé of how this prestigious investment firm really operates. His comments about how customers are viewed and treated is very revealing:

> I attend derivatives sales meetings where not one single minute is spent asking questions about how we

can help clients. It's purely about how we can make the most possible money off of them. If you were an alien from Mars and sat in on one of these meetings, you would believe that a client's success or progress was not part of the thought process at all. It makes me ill how callously people talk about ripping their clients off. Over the last 12 months I have seen five different managing directors refer to their own clients as "muppets," sometimes over internal e-mail. (Smith)

Most of the big investment firms have been engaged in sausage-making for a long time. They butcher real economic entities such as businesses and farms, grind up the by-products and squeeze them into little packages (tranches) with a lot of additives. They then sell these products to unsuspecting consumers, calling them such things as derivatives, structured asset backed securities, collateralized debt obligations, and the like. The strange names help disguise what they really are, kind of like using the term "sweetbreads" when serving people guts at a fancy dinner party. All of this is legal, of course, except when the products are laced with poison, which they often are. Like the meat packers that would buy sick or dead animals, these firms can chop up sick, dying businesses, repackage them into some type of obscure financial product, then purvey them to investors with promises of high returns. When this happened on a grand scale during the recent financial crisis, a lot of people got "cleaned out" in a massive bout of diarrhea.

The government did its best to investigate and appease an outraged public, but real reform is difficult when there is a revolving door between the policing agency and the firms it's supposed to be overseeing. High-ranking officials at the SEC commonly switch careers and start working for the big investment firms. Likewise, veteran directors at these firms will do a stint of public service at the SEC or other government agency after receiving their golden parachutes.

The best thing you can do as an investor is to avoid consuming the products these firms produce. Stick to the financial equivalent of organic, grass-fed beef raised by a rancher you trust. In other words, buy quality stocks of "healthy" companies run by competent and honest managers who distribute the majority of the profits back to the owners (i.e., the shareholders). If you want to buy bonds, buy real bonds from financially sound entities—not some artificial product that has been "cloned," "genetically modified," or "derived" from them.

Chapter 12

Sleaze and Fees

A prominent Hollywood actor found himself unable to spend a lot of time with his wife because of the demands of his job. Realizing that he was not adequately meeting her emotional needs, he asked his best friend to start spending some time with her. As all of us non-Hollywood people would have guessed, she ended up ditching her husband and running off with his best friend.

What seems obvious to most of us when it comes to relationships is often missed when it comes to finances. If you wouldn't hand over your wife or husband for someone else to "nurture," why would you do this with your money? Putting all of your savings into the hands of a trusted money manager is a really bad idea. He will either "run off with it" or start "dipping into it" by charging you fees.

If you don't have the time or the inclination to meet the emotional needs of your spouse, you shouldn't get married. If you don't have the time or the inclination to manage your savings, then you should either give them away or lock them away and forget about them. The first option might be a bit radical for those of us who don't aspire to sainthood. However, the second option is actually quite reasonable and relatively simple to do.

A lot of people feel that it is somehow irresponsible not to make high returns on their invested money. They should realize, however, that savings (which become investment capital when they are deployed into stocks or bonds) are only a catalyst for economic activity, rather than actual economic activity itself.

The management of your wealth, regardless of the amount, is a task that cannot be delegated to someone else any more than the management of your fitness can be delegated to someone else. Everyone can and should learn about saving and investing—and take charge of all the decision-making. Rather than handing over your assets to a hedge fund manager or financial planner, you should develop and implement your own conservative investment strategy. Managing your money well does not require a lot of time or an advanced degree in finance, just adherence to some basic, common sense principles.

Many people give up a significant portion of their investment returns in the form of fees paid to professionals to manage their money for them. Few of these professionals ever generate returns greater than that of a simple index fund. In fact, eighty percent of professional managers fail to beat the aggregate returns of all the stocks in the market, which an index fund replicates for a very low fee. Worse, they can lose a significant portion of your investment portfolio if they make the wrong calls; and if they are dishonest, they may take everything. The financial industry has succeeded in convincing a lot of hard-working successful people that they are incompetent to manage their own savings—that they should rely instead on the professionals trained by the financial industry. The reality is that most of the training these professionals receive is in marketing.

The analysts among them continually make predictions about whether or not the price of a stock will go up or down—something no one could possibly know. When some of them get it right—this always happens when people take different sides in a bet—investors eagerly hand over their funds to the winners in the belief that they are shrewd and insightful. Usually, they are just lucky. If their luck persists for a few years, they can often sucker in a large number of investors and continue betting with even bigger sums of money. At some point, though, almost all of them will end up losing, taking down their investors with them.

Why take such a risk with your hard-earned savings? Instead, you can simply put your funds into a few conventional investment vehicles, such as an index fund or bond fund at a large, well-established investment firm. Later, you can diversify into the stocks of a few solid, blue-chip companies that are profitable and pay a high dividend. Then you can (and should) forget about the markets and move on with your life. Periodically, you can check on things and possibly re-allocate some of your funds, but this will only rarely be necessary. Most people lose money when they try to predict what the economy, markets, and stock prices are going to do. This is, in fact, why hedge fund managers lose so much money—playing this game is their full-time job. The bottom line is that such predictions cannot be made reliably.

Therefore, it's better not to try. Instead of buying and selling all the time and stressing yourself out about whether or not you made the right decisions (and most of the time you won't), just invest in things that will steadily grow in value regardless of what happens in the markets. Yes, you will probably miss out on the higher returns being made by a few lucky winners—and these winners (whether they are prominent hedge fund managers or your colleagues at work) will be quite vocal about their recent good fortune. But for most of them, the good times will only be temporary and they will eventually start to experience losses—sometimes catastrophic losses. It is far better to stick to a sound investment plan that will generate moderate returns over the long run and that requires minimal oversight.

Chapter 13

Thanksgiving: The Rest of the Story

All of us vividly remember the traditional Thanksgiving story we learned in kindergarten. We may have even had to act out the various roles in a skit or play. Back then they didn't tell us the rest of the story—that those wonderful Wampanoag Indians living near Plymouth Rock eventually got whacked by their new friends. These Indians found out the hard way that generous hospitality and a "come one, come all" approach to foreigners isn't always the best policy if you're interested in protecting the wellbeing of your own community. Perhaps they should have just put up a big sign that said, "Welcome to America, Now Go Home."

Although generosity and helping the less fortunate is always a good thing, it must be approached carefully if you don't want to end up in the same (or worse) situation as those you are trying to help. One of the first rules taught to paramedics and emergency responders is not to put themselves or others in danger in their efforts to save someone. There is certainly some wiggle room with this rule, for which many a person having been rescued will be quite grateful, but the basic principle is valid. It is not fair to endanger an entire community to save a few unfortunate souls.

The United States has been very generous toward immigrants throughout its history. Sometimes the nation's policies have been guided by a genuine desire to help refugees from war-torn or impoverished countries. At other times, especially in recent years, immigration policies have been crafted to meet the need for cheap labor demanded by business interests.

The labor market, like the market for everything else in an economy, is driven by supply and demand. When there is strong demand and a short supply, business will have to offer higher wages to get people to quit what they are doing and come work for them. This is exactly what Henry Ford did back in the early part of the twentieth century. He built a big car factory to meet the huge demand for automobiles. But he needed a lot of people to work in the factory—more than were readily available in the Detroit area. There were plenty of farmers out in the hinterlands that had previously been content to stay put and work the land, even if they could only manage to eek out a lower class lifestyle by doing so.

Ford lured them off the land and into the factory by offering a previously unheard of $5 per day wage. New workers came in by the droves. Other manufacturers, not just those who made automobiles, were not very happy with Ford. He had now raised the bar and it would be nearly impossible to keep their existing employees without following suit. Higher wages allowed people to adopt a higher standard of living, and eventually America developed a very large middle class. In fact, America had a larger middle class than any other nation in the world. A large middle class fed economic growth, since more people were able to afford a greater variety of products. It also contributed to political stability, since most people felt like they had a real stake in things and wanted the system that they had benefitted from to keep running smoothly. Earlier in the century, Russia found out the hard way that a system which provided lavish wealth for a very few at the expense of large numbers of poor people was very unstable.

Throughout much of the twentieth century, America maintained a strong middle class and most people could find jobs that paid reasonably well. Eventually, however, things began to change. Many corporations started shifting their production overseas where wages were much cheaper. Even though the demand for labor was high, the supply (if it could be accessed from all over the world) was virtually unlimited. And since lots of really, really poor people would be competing with each other for the jobs, corporations could go with the cheapest bid. Since American workers were accustomed to much higher wages (and needed more income to maintain a reasonable standard of living in a First World industrialized nation), they never had a chance.

Local business owners, however, were kind of stuck. There were certain things that just couldn't be shipped overseas—things like cooking hamburgers, cutting grass, and cleaning houses. A lot of the nation's displaced factory workers still had a shot at obtaining well-paying, though perhaps less interesting, jobs in the service sector. But the business owners were very shrewd. If they couldn't ship production overseas, they would bring the cheap labor here. By pressuring government leaders to open up the borders and relax enforcement of existing immigration laws, they could count on a virtually unlimited supply of eager workers from Latin America who would be willing do the jobs that Americans were "unwilling to do" for such a cheap price. Thus, much of America's middle class is slipping into the ranks of the poor. An unstable political system is gradually developing which is controlled by a small number of very rich people. Unless things change, the prospects for the average worker in America are not very good. Even white collar professionals, such as computer programmers and engineers, are starting to feel the effects as more and more of these jobs are shipped offshore to places like India and China.

For American Indians, Thanksgiving has never been one of their favorite holidays. If current trends continue, it may lose much of its appeal for the rest of us as well. Perhaps the Chinese New Year or Cinco de Mayo will take its place.

Chapter 14

Housing Hokum

Many Americans are hanging on to the hope that a recovery in the housing market will somehow drive a broader economic recovery that will put us back on a pathway toward ever-growing national prosperity. Yet the very first Americans (the Indians, that is) would have been quite perplexed by such a strange idea. If some white settler had shown up and told them that if they would just build a lot of teepees, everyone in the tribe would stay warm, well-fed, well-clothed, and decked out in the latest headdresses and turquoise jewelry, they would immediately have suspected that he had been taking some "bad medicine."

They knew very well that tribal prosperity was first and foremost dependent upon good hunting grounds and farmlands. Teepees didn't magically lure a bunch of buffalo into the area. In primitive and modern societies, people build houses in order to remain near the source of their economic livelihood, not as a means of creating it when it doesn't already exist. Americans will start prospering once again when they start making things that others want to buy and doing things that others are willing to pay for. In the 21st century that means we're going to have to be really good at math, science, and engineering. If the only things we know how to make are Snuggies and Frappaccinos, and the only things we know how to do are flip burgers and greet people coming through the door at Walmart, we can forget about a recovery in the housing sector. It's time to dispense with all this hokum about building our economic recovery on the housing market and focus instead on developing a highly educated and skilled workforce that will revitalize our manufacturing sector so that we can compete in the global economy.

A few enlightened politicians have publicly addressed this urgent need, but they don't seem to be able to do much about it. You can always vote for the good guys and hope that things will eventually turn around. In the meantime, it's best to prepare yourself for economic survival in case the rosier predictions don't materialize. How can you do this? By learning as much as you can and developing a skill set that you can charge money for. Knowing how to build teepees or sell them to other members of the community is probably not going to be a reliable way to put meat on the table. So if you are a contractor, real estate agent, or interior decorator, you would be wise to start learning how to hunt. In the modern world that means developing the technical skills that the current job market demands. Unfortunately, your options may be somewhat limited.

Healthcare always seems to offer pretty good prospects, since whenever other people in the community get sick, they will generally spend whatever is necessary to get better rather than put the money into a new television set or couch. Since all the easy loans dried up and people can't run out and buy a new house once things start breaking, you may be able to make a good living by learning how to fix things that most people can't fix themselves, such as broken pipes and faulty wiring. If you're after the bigger game of the white collar variety, there will be few options other than spending a lot of years getting a good education in a marketable field.

Chapter 15

Student Loans: Leave Them Alone!

Two types of debt have traditionally been viewed positively by our society: mortgage debt and school debt. After the excesses of the real estate boom and the ensuing financial crisis, mortgage debt is starting to be regarded with more suspicion. School debt, on the other hand, is still considered by many to be a necessary and worthy means of obtaining an education and building a productive career.

In previous centuries it would have been very difficult to find a lot of investors willing to fork over their capital to pay for someone's schooling in the hope that this person would then pay them back with interest after landing a lucrative job. They wanted guarantees. There was, however, a good analog for the current debt-financed career pathway that begins in the colleges. In those days, the pathway started in Europe and ended in the New World. Rich people would pay for your passage across the ocean if you committed to paying them back with your labor for a certain number of years—typically 3 to 7.

If you happened to land a job with a nice guy, he might treat you well and give you a gold watch and a retirement party at the end of your stint. However, if you ended up with a jerk, you were in big trouble. Some of these "masters" could be very abusive, beating their servants, overworking them, and even refusing to let them leave after their term of service was complete.

Indentured servitude has fallen out of favor in America, unless you are an immigrant who has been smuggled in illegally from China. Nevertheless, there are many parallels with the current student loan system. You take on debt—sometimes enormous debt—in the hope that you will find lucrative employment in the new world where you will presumably arrive after an arduous journey through college. In the past, it was a pretty good gig for some people. Nowadays, however, more and more students—like their unlucky predecessors a few centuries ago—are finding out that they got a raw deal. If they can even find a job, it's low pay and they're going to be stuck paying off this debt for the rest of their lives.

Indentured servants had little hope of appealing to a benevolent government to rescue them from their tribulation. Kings and their officials were decidedly business-friendly. Nothing much has changed today. In 2005 Congress enacted much stricter bankruptcy laws that made private student loans non-dischargeable. So if you really run into hard times, you can potentially get rid of most of the debt hanging over your head (even casino debt) and get a new start. But forget about eliminating those student loans—you'll take them with you to the grave. The interest payments will constitute a continuous draw on any money you'll ever make, dragging you down into a lower standard of living and keeping you there for the rest of your life.

All of this is not to say that school is not a good investment. It's absolutely the best investment you can make with your surplus funds. But classes, like stocks, should never be purchased with money that you don't have. From time to time, articles appear on the Internet claiming that college isn't worth the price you pay for it, since you can often make more money going straight into the job market right after high school. But the goal of college should be to get an education, not get a job, and an education will add value to our lives even if it doesn't open up a pathway to lucrative employment. Claiming that education isn't worth it is like claiming that a healthy diet isn't worth it—it's cheaper to go ahead and eat junk food and just pay the medical bills!

Education, like quality food, is always worth the price—and if we shop around, we can often find some pretty good deals that don't require taking out a loan. Community colleges, even with the recent tuition increases, still offer a pretty good bang for the buck. If you need to delay enrollment while you save money for the registration fees, you can always get a jump start on things by heading down to the local library. Abraham Lincoln figured out that even if you couldn't afford to pay for an education, you could still get one by reading books.

Chapter 16

Don't Bet The Farm

Bill was a successful retail executive for a large supermarket chain. He and his family lived in a nice home that was completely paid for. He also owned a vacation home at the beach. His children grew up with nice clothes, toys and all the other things that prosperous parents typically want to provide for their offspring. Everything was on track for an early retirement and years of relaxing at the beach. Then he had a stroke.

At first, he was completely paralyzed on his left side and couldn't walk. Eventually he recovered some movement and became ambulatory again. Not wanting to skip a beat, he got right back to work. Yet because of his limitations, the company ended up firing him. He applied at numerous other companies, but no one wanted to give him a job. So he decided he would launch out and go for a big dream he had been keeping in his bucket list for a long time: to start his own hardware store. It took everything he had—all of his savings and a big line of credit—but in the end he was able to establish the largest and most beautiful hardware store he had ever seen. But this wasn't the end, it was just the beginning—of a stagnant economy, relentless bill collectors, unabated stress, and an eventual collapse of the entire venture. He would now be starting a whole new life, setting out in an entirely new direction into unknown territory—physically handicapped, tired, and with nothing but the shirt on his back.

Perhaps Bill will one day meet with good fortune all over again and his story will be picked up by some motivational speaker or published in a new volume of *Chicken Soup For The Soul*. The odds are, however, that his life will steadily decline into deeper, darker depths of poverty and pain. Like the rest of us, he's no Benjamin Button and he's not getting any younger, healthier, or energetic. If this all sounds very depressing, it is.

Bill, like so many others who have been deluded by the success stories peddled in the popular press, thought he could bet the farm and win. The reality is that savings takes a lifetime to accumulate. Unless you are a cat and have eight more chances to get it right, betting everything you have on a business venture is virtually guaranteed to end in disaster. Eighty percent of all new business ventures fail—no matter who attempts them. If your dream is to start a new business then set aside a certain amount of money for that purpose, but don't raid your retirement fund—no matter how certain you may be that your new business idea is a sure bet.

Chapter 17

How To Avoid Getting Hacked, Jacked, or Whacked: A Brief Guide to Personal Financial Security

"Show and Tell" has always been a favorite activity for kids of kindergarten age. A lot of adults like to play too—and some of them have some pretty cool stuff to show off. Others are content to tell the world about how much money they've made. Some of the richest will gladly offer details to magazines like *Forbes* so they can be published in one of their lists. In Mexico, this practice is less popular, since it can easily lead to getting an ear chopped off by a band of kidnappers.

The bad guys in the US have traditionally been a bit nicer, but they still make good use of the free information offered to them by their targets. When the famous bank robber Willie Sutton was asked why he chose to rob banks, he famously responded, "because that's where the money is." Though such criminals are clearly lacking in certain elements of common sense because of the lifestyle they have chosen, they are by no means completely impaired. They can still spot the obvious.

It should come as no surprise, therefore, that one of the best ways to deter criminals is not to dangle valuables in front of them. Even taking this first simple step will significantly improve your chances of not becoming a victim. If you really must have the big house, fancy cars, and fine jewelry, you'd better take some precautions and live in a guarded, gated community and avoid any excursions to the other side of the tracks.

If you have something that someone else wants, and that person doesn't have any scruples, then it is prudent to take some simple steps to protect yourself. The danger isn't just limited to your money and your goods, because as long as you are connected to them in some way, someone may just decide to take you out of the way.

In addition to avoiding displays of material wealth, it is very important to limit information about your financial wealth. Keeping mum about business or investment successes will give us an added margin of safety, though our inner child will be squirming with the urge to blurt things out. If we are successful enough to draw media coverage, playing things down will be even more difficult. What kid could ever pass up the opportunity to get his picture in the paper if he accomplished something noteworthy? Yet anything that finds its way into the media finds its way into Google; and yes, criminals know how to use Google too.

The sharper tools in the shed can even hack into your computer, planting a virus or worm that will send back financial information such as bank account numbers and passwords. If you have online access to your bank accounts, you should check them regularly and balance them religiously to make sure you haven't inadvertently wired a substantial amount of money to the Cayman Islands. Checking credit card receipts against the statement will alert you to that monthly $1.99 charge that has no explanation. The guy over in Russia makes a killing when a million people like you assume it must have been for a cup of coffee that you just forgot about. When you see the big charge for the platinum jewelry from *Nieman Marcus*, you can call up the fraud center at the credit card company and get a refund. Wait two months and all bets are off.

Checking the phone bill is also miserable necessity as well. Thieves don't just steal money and goods, they also steal services. They can tap into your phone number and charge up a lot of calls to their mother-in-law who lives in Nigeria. Speaking of Nigeria, if a lawyer with poor grammar skills sends you an email asking you to deposit a sum of money into a certain bank account so he can send you a lot more money that belongs to a dead rich guy, don't do it. He's lying.

Hacking is above the pay grade of most criminals, so they resort to something easier—dumpster diving. If you throw away anything besides the junk mail without shredding it, these bottom feeders will have access to lots of useful information—names, addresses, organizations you belong to, letters with your signature on them, bank account numbers, and your social security number (printed on tax returns which a lot of really organized people throw out every three years). All they have to do is bring the good stuff back to the smart guy who gives them their drug money and he'll be able to connect all the dots so he can take out a line of credit in your name.

Protecting yourself, your family, and your assets requires some forethought and the consistent implementation of certain protocols, but in the end the time and effort invested will be well worth it.

Works Cited

AFL-CIO. "Employees Left Behind." 23 June 2004. <http://www.aflcio.org/corporateamerica/enron/employees.cfm>.

———. "Long-Term Trends in CEO and Worker Pay." 23 June 2004. < http://www.aflcio.org/corporateamerica/paywatch/retirement security/index.cfm>.

———. "The Enron Story." 23 June 2004. <http://www.aflcio.org/corporateamerica/enron/story.cfm>.

FOXNews. "Timeline: Enron Corporation." 28 December 2005. 10 June 2013. <http://www.foxnews.com/story>. 0%2C2933%2C39655%2C00.html

HoustonChronicle. "Enron Timeline." 17 January 2002. 23 June 2004. <http://www.chron.com/cs/CDA/story.hts/special/enron/1127125>.

Araghi, Farshad A. "Global Depeasantization, 1945-1990." *The Sociological Quarterly* Vol.36 (No.2): 337-368.

———. *Social Change Lecture Series.* FAU Broward Campus. Ft. Lauderdale, May/June 1997.

———. Forthcoming. "The World Bank and the Third World Agriculture: A Review of *Faith and Credit, Mortgaging the Earth*, and *50 Years Is Enough*." *Contemporary Sociology.*

Armario, Christine. "1 in 4 American children raised by a single parent." 27 April 2011. 8 June 2013. <http://www.today.com/id/42780551/ns/today-

today_health/t/american-children-raised-single-parent/#.UbOLaJUd6rc>.

Arrighi, Giovanni. *The Long Twentieth Century: Money, Power, and the Origins of Our Times*. London: Verso, 1994.

Bandow, Doug. "The Case for a *Much* Smaller Military" *Fortune*. June 23, 1997.

Barlett, Donald L., and James B. Steele. *America:Who Really Pays The Taxes*. New York: Simon & Schuster.

Baumohl, Bernard. "The Best of Times?" *TIME* July 28, 1997: 54.

Conan, Neil. "Analysis: Executive compensation and whether CEOs are worth millions of dollars," *Talk of the Nation*, transcript of live radio broadcast (Washington, D.C.: National Public Radio, 7 October 2002).

Corn, David. "SECRET VIDEO: Romney Tells Millionaire Donors What He REALLY Thinks of Obama Voters." 6 June 2013. <http://www.motherjones.com/politics/2012/09/secret-video-romney-private-fundraiser>.

Fonda, Daren and Daniel Kadlec, "The Rumble Over Executive Pay." *TIME*, 31 May 2004, 63.

George, Susan. *The Debt Boomerang*. London: Pluto Press, 1992.

Greenberg, Jerald. *Managing Behavior in Organizations*, 4th ed. Upper Saddle River, New Jersey: Pearson Prentice Hall, 2005.

Hauchler, Ingomar, and Paul M. Kennedy. *Global Trends: The World Almanac Of Development and Peace*. New York: Continuum, 1994.

Hanley, Charles J. "Studies: Iraq Costs US $12B Per

Month." 10 March 2008. 6 June 2013 <http://www.huffingtonpost.com/2008/03/10/studies-iraq-costs-us-12b_n_90694.html>.

Inequality.org. "Income Inequality." 6 June 2013. <http://inequality.org/income-inequality/>

Jaschik, Scott. "Murky Picture For Faculty Salaries." *Inside Higher Ed*. 13 April 2009. 10 June 2013. <http://www.insidehighered.com/news/2009/04/13/aaup>.

Knoke, William. *Bold New World* New York: Kodansha America, 1996.

Lappe, Frances Moore, and Joseph Collins. *World Hunger: Twelve Myths*. New York: Grove Weidenfeld, 1986.

_____. *Taking Population Seriously*. San Francisco: The Institute For Food and Development Policy, 1988.

Londoño, Earnesto. "Iraq, Afghan wars will cost to $4 trillion to $6 trillion, Harvard study says." 28 March 2013. 6 June 2013. <http://articles.washingtonpost.com/2013-03-28/world/38097452_1_iraq-price-tag-first-gulf-war-veterans>.

Mann, Donald. "A Monthly Commentary on Population and Immigration Issues." *The NPG Journal*: Vol. 5, No 3, 6 February 2012. 16 April 2013. <http://www.npg.org/npgjournalv5n3.html>.

Marx, Karl, and Frederick Engels. "The Manifesto of the Communist Party."*Readings In Social Theory*. Ed. James Farganis. New York: McGraw-Hill, 1996.

Murphy, Kevin J. "Executive Compensation," *Handbook of Labor Economics*, eds. Orley Ashenfelter and David Card, vol. 3 (North Holland, 1999), 9-24.

Orhanghazi, Ozgur. "The Global Unemployment Crisis." 30 March 2013. 6 June 2013. <http://www.truth-out.org/news/item/15428-the-global-unemployment-crisis>.

Pollard, Sidney, ed. 1990. *Wealth &Poverty: An Economic History of the Twentieth Century.* Oxford: Oxford University Press.

Papademetriou, Demetrios G. "The Global Struggle with Illegal Immigration: No End In Sight." September 2005. 6 June 2013. <http://www.migrationinformation.org/feature/display.cfm?ID=336>.

Reingold, Jennifer. "Executive Pay: It continues to explode—and options alone are creating paper billionaires." *Businessweek*, 17 April 2000, 2-3. 23 June 2004. <http://www.businessweek.com:2000/00_16/b3677014.htm>.

Ritzer, George. *Sociological Theory.* Fourth ed. New York: McGraw-Hill, 1996.

Schwartz, Nelson D. "The Infinity Pool of Executive Pay." 6 April 2013. 8 June 2013. <http://www.nytimes.com/2013/04/07/business/executive-pay-shows-modest-2012-gain-but-oh-those-perks.html?pagewanted=all&_r=0>.

Sinclair, Upton. *The Jungle.* Available at *The Literature Network.* 10 June 2013. <http://www.online-literature.com/upton_sinclair/jungle/>.

Smith, Greg. "Why I Am Leaving Goldman Sachs." 14 March 2012. 10 June 2013. <http://www.nytimes.com/2012/03/14/opinion/why-i-am-leaving-goldman-sachs.html?pagewanted=all&_r=0>

Joseph E. Stiglitz, Joseph E. "The Economic

Consequences of Mr. Bush." December 2007. 6 June <http://www.vanityfair.com/politics/features/2007/12/bush200712>.

Taylor, Timothy. 2008. *America and the New Global Economy*. The Teaching Company. Audio File.

About The Author

Foster Stanback is a managing partner at various domestic and international firms engaged in business activities that include shipping, distribution, retail sales, and real estate. He has been an active investor in international equities markets for over two decades. He holds an M.A. in Sociology from Florida Atlantic University, where he received a distinguished alumnus award in 2011. He also holds an M.A. in Religion from Pepperdine University, an M.A. in Psychology from the Pepperdine Graduate School of Education and Psychology, and an M.S. in Marketing and Technology Innovation from the Worcester Polytechnic Institute. In 2010 he was inducted into the Beta Gamma Sigma International Honor Society for Collegiate Schools of Business.

www.ingramcontent.com/pod-product-compliance
Lightning Source LLC
Chambersburg PA
CBHW070234180526
45158CB00001BA/503